C-997   CAREER EXAMINATION SERIES

*This is your
PASSBOOK for...*

Senior Building Custodian

*Test Preparation Study Guide
Questions & Answers*

COPYRIGHT NOTICE

This book is SOLELY intended for, is sold ONLY to, and its use is RESTRICTED to individual, bona fide applicants or candidates who qualify by virtue of having seriously filed applications for appropriate license, certificate, professional and/or promotional advancement, higher school matriculation, scholarship, or other legitimate requirements of education and/or governmental authorities.

This book is NOT intended for use, class instruction, tutoring, training, duplication, copying, reprinting, excerption, or adaptation, etc., by:

1) Other publishers
2) Proprietors and/or Instructors of "Coaching" and/or Preparatory Courses
3) Personnel and/or Training Divisions of commercial, industrial, and governmental organizations
4) Schools, colleges, or universities and/or their departments and staffs, including teachers and other personnel
5) Testing Agencies or Bureaus
6) Study groups which seek by the purchase of a single volume to copy and/or duplicate and/or adapt this material for use by the group as a whole without having purchased individual volumes for each of the members of the group
7) Et al.

Such persons would be in violation of appropriate Federal and State statutes.

PROVISION OF LICENSING AGREEMENTS – Recognized educational, commercial, industrial, and governmental institutions and organizations, and others legitimately engaged in educational pursuits, including training, testing, and measurement activities, may address request for a licensing agreement to the copyright owners, who will determine whether, and under what conditions, including fees and charges, the materials in this book may be used them. In other words, a licensing facility exists for the legitimate use of the material in this book on other than an individual basis. However, it is asseverated and affirmed here that the material in this book CANNOT be used without the receipt of the express permission of such a licensing agreement from the Publishers. Inquiries re licensing should be addressed to the company, attention rights and permissions department.

All rights reserved, including the right of reproduction in whole or in part, in any form or by any means, electronic or mechanical, including photocopying, recording, or by any information storage and retrieval system, without permission in writing from the Publisher.

Copyright © 2024 by
National Learning Corporation

212 Michael Drive, Syosset, NY 11791
(516) 921-8888 • www.passbooks.com
E-mail: info@passbooks.com

PASSBOOK® SERIES

THE *PASSBOOK® SERIES* has been created to prepare applicants and candidates for the ultimate academic battlefield – the examination room.

At some time in our lives, each and every one of us may be required to take an examination – for validation, matriculation, admission, qualification, registration, certification, or licensure.

Based on the assumption that every applicant or candidate has met the basic formal educational standards, has taken the required number of courses, and read the necessary texts, the *PASSBOOK® SERIES* furnishes the one special preparation which may assure passing with confidence, instead of failing with insecurity. Examination questions – together with answers – are furnished as the basic vehicle for study so that the mysteries of the examination and its compounding difficulties may be eliminated or diminished by a sure method.

This book is meant to help you pass your examination provided that you qualify and are serious in your objective.

The entire field is reviewed through the huge store of content information which is succinctly presented through a provocative and challenging approach – the question-and-answer method.

A climate of success is established by furnishing the correct answers at the end of each test.

You soon learn to recognize types of questions, forms of questions, and patterns of questioning. You may even begin to anticipate expected outcomes.

You perceive that many questions are repeated or adapted so that you can gain acute insights, which may enable you to score many sure points.

You learn how to confront new questions, or types of questions, and to attack them confidently and work out the correct answers.

You note objectives and emphases, and recognize pitfalls and dangers, so that you may make positive educational adjustments.

Moreover, you are kept fully informed in relation to new concepts, methods, practices, and directions in the field.

You discover that you are actually taking the examination all the time: you are preparing for the examination by "taking" an examination, not by reading extraneous and/or supererogatory textbooks.

In short, this PASSBOOK®, used directedly, should be an important factor in helping you to pass your test.

SENIOR BUILDING CUSTODIAN

DUTIES
Under general supervision, performs work of a highly difficult and responsible nature in the supervision of the cleaning and maintaining of public buildings and their immediate grounds and in the enforcement of safety requirements. Performs related work.

EXAMPLES OF TYPICAL TASKS
Is responsible for the cleanliness and maintenance of public buildings entailing supervision of a large group of subordinate employees, such as building custodians, assistant building custodians, elevator operators, cleaners, watchmen, window cleaners, etc., engaged in sweeping, dusting, scrubbing, mopping, polishing, gathering and disposing of refuse, operating a heating plant, mowing and caring for lawns, and operating elevators, or may be assistant to the Supervisor of Building Custodians. Inspects building to note general condition and necessity for repairs. Inspects work of subordinates to insure maximum efficiency, economy and quality of work; supervises or participates in the operation of a steam boiler heating system; performs and supervises cleaning activities; assigns tasks to subordinates and gives instructions in the use of building cleaning supplies, materials, and equipment; makes minor carpentry, plumbing, electrical, and other building repairs; cleans or supervises the cleaning of boilers; inspects boiler system for defects and makes necessary repairs; varnishes desks and chairs and paints lavatories, fire escapes, and doors; requisitions supplies as required; checks fire alarm system to insure proper operation in emergency; refills fire extinguishers; performs a variety of custodial activities as required. Requisitions stock and issues supplies. Trains and arranges for training of new employees. Prepares work schedules. Maintains records and prepares required reports.

SCOPE OF EXAMINATION
The written test will be designed to test for knowledge, skills, and/or abilities in such areas as:
1. Building cleaning;
2. Building operation and maintenance;
3. Ability to read and follow written instructions;
4. Arithmetical reasoning; and
5. Supervision.

HOW TO TAKE A TEST

I. YOU MUST PASS AN EXAMINATION

A. WHAT EVERY CANDIDATE SHOULD KNOW

Examination applicants often ask us for help in preparing for the written test. What can I study in advance? What kinds of questions will be asked? How will the test be given? How will the papers be graded?

As an applicant for a civil service examination, you may be wondering about some of these things. Our purpose here is to suggest effective methods of advance study and to describe civil service examinations.

Your chances for success on this examination can be increased if you know how to prepare. Those "pre-examination jitters" can be reduced if you know what to expect. You can even experience an adventure in good citizenship if you know why civil service exams are given.

B. WHY ARE CIVIL SERVICE EXAMINATIONS GIVEN?

Civil service examinations are important to you in two ways. As a citizen, you want public jobs filled by employees who know how to do their work. As a job seeker, you want a fair chance to compete for that job on an equal footing with other candidates. The best-known means of accomplishing this two-fold goal is the competitive examination.

Exams are widely publicized throughout the nation. They may be administered for jobs in federal, state, city, municipal, town or village governments or agencies.

Any citizen may apply, with some limitations, such as the age or residence of applicants. Your experience and education may be reviewed to see whether you meet the requirements for the particular examination. When these requirements exist, they are reasonable and applied consistently to all applicants. Thus, a competitive examination may cause you some uneasiness now, but it is your privilege and safeguard.

C. HOW ARE CIVIL SERVICE EXAMS DEVELOPED?

Examinations are carefully written by trained technicians who are specialists in the field known as "psychological measurement," in consultation with recognized authorities in the field of work that the test will cover. These experts recommend the subject matter areas or skills to be tested; only those knowledges or skills important to your success on the job are included. The most reliable books and source materials available are used as references. Together, the experts and technicians judge the difficulty level of the questions.

Test technicians know how to phrase questions so that the problem is clearly stated. Their ethics do not permit "trick" or "catch" questions. Questions may have been tried out on sample groups, or subjected to statistical analysis, to determine their usefulness.

Written tests are often used in combination with performance tests, ratings of training and experience, and oral interviews. All of these measures combine to form the best-known means of finding the right person for the right job.

II. HOW TO PASS THE WRITTEN TEST

A. NATURE OF THE EXAMINATION

To prepare intelligently for civil service examinations, you should know how they differ from school examinations you have taken. In school you were assigned certain definite pages to read or subjects to cover. The examination questions were quite detailed and usually emphasized memory. Civil service exams, on the other hand, try to discover your present ability to perform the duties of a position, plus your potentiality to learn these duties. In other words, a civil service exam attempts to predict how successful you will be. Questions cover such a broad area that they cannot be as minute and detailed as school exam questions.

In the public service similar kinds of work, or positions, are grouped together in one "class." This process is known as *position-classification*. All the positions in a class are paid according to the salary range for that class. One class title covers all of these positions, and they are all tested by the same examination.

B. FOUR BASIC STEPS

1) Study the announcement

How, then, can you know what subjects to study? Our best answer is: "Learn as much as possible about the class of positions for which you've applied." The exam will test the knowledge, skills and abilities needed to do the work.

Your most valuable source of information about the position you want is the official exam announcement. This announcement lists the training and experience qualifications. Check these standards and apply only if you come reasonably close to meeting them.

The brief description of the position in the examination announcement offers some clues to the subjects which will be tested. Think about the job itself. Review the duties in your mind. Can you perform them, or are there some in which you are rusty? Fill in the blank spots in your preparation.

Many jurisdictions preview the written test in the exam announcement by including a section called "Knowledge and Abilities Required," "Scope of the Examination," or some similar heading. Here you will find out specifically what fields will be tested.

2) Review your own background

Once you learn in general what the position is all about, and what you need to know to do the work, ask yourself which subjects you already know fairly well and which need improvement. You may wonder whether to concentrate on improving your strong areas or on building some background in your fields of weakness. When the announcement has specified "some knowledge" or "considerable knowledge," or has used adjectives like "beginning principles of…" or "advanced … methods," you can get a clue as to the number and difficulty of questions to be asked in any given field. More questions, and hence broader coverage, would be included for those subjects which are more important in the work. Now weigh your strengths and weaknesses against the job requirements and prepare accordingly.

3) Determine the level of the position

Another way to tell how intensively you should prepare is to understand the level of the job for which you are applying. Is it the entering level? In other words, is this the position in which beginners in a field of work are hired? Or is it an intermediate or advanced level? Sometimes this is indicated by such words as "Junior" or "Senior" in the class title. Other jurisdictions use Roman numerals to designate the level – Clerk I, Clerk II, for example. The word "Supervisor" sometimes appears in the title. If the level is not indicated by the title, check the description of duties. Will you be working under very close supervision, or will you have responsibility for independent decisions in this work?

4) Choose appropriate study materials

Now that you know the subjects to be examined and the relative amount of each subject to be covered, you can choose suitable study materials. For beginning level jobs, or even advanced ones, if you have a pronounced weakness in some aspect of your training, read a modern, standard textbook in that field. Be sure it is up to date and has general coverage. Such books are normally available at your library, and the librarian will be glad to help you locate one. For entry-level positions, questions of appropriate difficulty are chosen – neither highly advanced questions, nor those too simple. Such questions require careful thought but not advanced training.

If the position for which you are applying is technical or advanced, you will read more advanced, specialized material. If you are already familiar with the basic principles of your field, elementary textbooks would waste your time. Concentrate on advanced textbooks and technical periodicals. Think through the concepts and review difficult problems in your field.

These are all general sources. You can get more ideas on your own initiative, following these leads. For example, training manuals and publications of the government agency which employs workers in your field can be useful, particularly for technical and professional positions. A letter or visit to the government department involved may result in more specific study suggestions, and certainly will provide you with a more definite idea of the exact nature of the position you are seeking.

III. KINDS OF TESTS

Tests are used for purposes other than measuring knowledge and ability to perform specified duties. For some positions, it is equally important to test ability to make adjustments to new situations or to profit from training. In others, basic mental abilities not dependent on information are essential. Questions which test these things may not appear as pertinent to the duties of the position as those which test for knowledge and information. Yet they are often highly important parts of a fair examination. For very general questions, it is almost impossible to help you direct your study efforts. What we can do is to point out some of the more common of these general abilities needed in public service positions and describe some typical questions.

1) General information

Broad, general information has been found useful for predicting job success in some kinds of work. This is tested in a variety of ways, from vocabulary lists to questions about current events. Basic background in some field of work, such as sociology or economics, may be sampled in a group of questions. Often these are principles which have become familiar to most persons through exposure rather than through formal training. It is difficult to advise you how to study for these questions; being alert to the world around you is our best suggestion.

2) Verbal ability

An example of an ability needed in many positions is verbal or language ability. Verbal ability is, in brief, the ability to use and understand words. Vocabulary and grammar tests are typical measures of this ability. Reading comprehension or paragraph interpretation questions are common in many kinds of civil service tests. You are given a paragraph of written material and asked to find its central meaning.

3) **Numerical ability**

Number skills can be tested by the familiar arithmetic problem, by checking paired lists of numbers to see which are alike and which are different, or by interpreting charts and graphs. In the latter test, a graph may be printed in the test booklet which you are asked to use as the basis for answering questions.

4) **Observation**

A popular test for law-enforcement positions is the observation test. A picture is shown to you for several minutes, then taken away. Questions about the picture test your ability to observe both details and larger elements.

5) **Following directions**

In many positions in the public service, the employee must be able to carry out written instructions dependably and accurately. You may be given a chart with several columns, each column listing a variety of information. The questions require you to carry out directions involving the information given in the chart.

6) **Skills and aptitudes**

Performance tests effectively measure some manual skills and aptitudes. When the skill is one in which you are trained, such as typing or shorthand, you can practice. These tests are often very much like those given in business school or high school courses. For many of the other skills and aptitudes, however, no short-time preparation can be made. Skills and abilities natural to you or that you have developed throughout your lifetime are being tested.

Many of the general questions just described provide all the data needed to answer the questions and ask you to use your reasoning ability to find the answers. Your best preparation for these tests, as well as for tests of facts and ideas, is to be at your physical and mental best. You, no doubt, have your own methods of getting into an exam-taking mood and keeping "in shape." The next section lists some ideas on this subject.

IV. KINDS OF QUESTIONS

Only rarely is the "essay" question, which you answer in narrative form, used in civil service tests. Civil service tests are usually of the short-answer type. Full instructions for answering these questions will be given to you at the examination. But in case this is your first experience with short-answer questions and separate answer sheets, here is what you need to know:

1) **Multiple-choice Questions**

Most popular of the short-answer questions is the "multiple choice" or "best answer" question. It can be used, for example, to test for factual knowledge, ability to solve problems or judgment in meeting situations found at work.

A multiple-choice question is normally one of three types—
- It can begin with an incomplete statement followed by several possible endings. You are to find the one ending which *best* completes the statement, although some of the others may not be entirely wrong.
- It can also be a complete statement in the form of a question which is answered by choosing one of the statements listed.

- It can be in the form of a problem – again you select the best answer.

Here is an example of a multiple-choice question with a discussion which should give you some clues as to the method for choosing the right answer:

When an employee has a complaint about his assignment, the action which will *best* help him overcome his difficulty is to
- A. discuss his difficulty with his coworkers
- B. take the problem to the head of the organization
- C. take the problem to the person who gave him the assignment
- D. say nothing to anyone about his complaint

In answering this question, you should study each of the choices to find which is best. Consider choice "A" – Certainly an employee may discuss his complaint with fellow employees, but no change or improvement can result, and the complaint remains unresolved. Choice "B" is a poor choice since the head of the organization probably does not know what assignment you have been given, and taking your problem to him is known as "going over the head" of the supervisor. The supervisor, or person who made the assignment, is the person who can clarify it or correct any injustice. Choice "C" is, therefore, correct. To say nothing, as in choice "D," is unwise. Supervisors have and interest in knowing the problems employees are facing, and the employee is seeking a solution to his problem.

2) True/False Questions

The "true/false" or "right/wrong" form of question is sometimes used. Here a complete statement is given. Your job is to decide whether the statement is right or wrong.

SAMPLE: A roaming cell-phone call to a nearby city costs less than a non-roaming call to a distant city.

This statement is wrong, or false, since roaming calls are more expensive.

This is not a complete list of all possible question forms, although most of the others are variations of these common types. You will always get complete directions for answering questions. Be sure you understand *how* to mark your answers – ask questions until you do.

V. RECORDING YOUR ANSWERS

Computer terminals are used more and more today for many different kinds of exams.
For an examination with very few applicants, you may be told to record your answers in the test booklet itself. Separate answer sheets are much more common. If this separate answer sheet is to be scored by machine – and this is often the case – it is highly important that you mark your answers correctly in order to get credit.
An electronic scoring machine is often used in civil service offices because of the speed with which papers can be scored. Machine-scored answer sheets must be marked with a pencil, which will be given to you. This pencil has a high graphite content which responds to the electronic scoring machine. As a matter of fact, stray dots may register as answers, so do not let your pencil rest on the answer sheet while you are pondering the correct answer. Also, if your pencil lead breaks or is otherwise defective, ask for another.

Since the answer sheet will be dropped in a slot in the scoring machine, be careful not to bend the corners or get the paper crumpled.

The answer sheet normally has five vertical columns of numbers, with 30 numbers to a column. These numbers correspond to the question numbers in your test booklet. After each number, going across the page are four or five pairs of dotted lines. These short dotted lines have small letters or numbers above them. The first two pairs may also have a "T" or "F" above the letters. This indicates that the first two pairs only are to be used if the questions are of the true-false type. If the questions are multiple choice, disregard the "T" and "F" and pay attention only to the small letters or numbers.

Answer your questions in the manner of the sample that follows:

32. The largest city in the United States is
    A. Washington, D.C.
    B. New York City
    C. Chicago
    D. Detroit
    E. San Francisco

1) Choose the answer you think is best. (New York City is the largest, so "B" is correct.)
2) Find the row of dotted lines numbered the same as the question you are answering. (Find row number 32)
3) Find the pair of dotted lines corresponding to the answer. (Find the pair of lines under the mark "B.")
4) Make a solid black mark between the dotted lines.

VI. BEFORE THE TEST

Common sense will help you find procedures to follow to get ready for an examination. Too many of us, however, overlook these sensible measures. Indeed, nervousness and fatigue have been found to be the most serious reasons why applicants fail to do their best on civil service tests. Here is a list of reminders:

- Begin your preparation early – Don't wait until the last minute to go scurrying around for books and materials or to find out what the position is all about.
- Prepare continuously – An hour a night for a week is better than an all-night cram session. This has been definitely established. What is more, a night a week for a month will return better dividends than crowding your study into a shorter period of time.
- Locate the place of the exam – You have been sent a notice telling you when and where to report for the examination. If the location is in a different town or otherwise unfamiliar to you, it would be well to inquire the best route and learn something about the building.
- Relax the night before the test – Allow your mind to rest. Do not study at all that night. Plan some mild recreation or diversion; then go to bed early and get a good night's sleep.
- Get up early enough to make a leisurely trip to the place for the test – This way unforeseen events, traffic snarls, unfamiliar buildings, etc. will not upset you.
- Dress comfortably – A written test is not a fashion show. You will be known by number and not by name, so wear something comfortable.

- Leave excess paraphernalia at home – Shopping bags and odd bundles will get in your way. You need bring only the items mentioned in the official notice you received; usually everything you need is provided. Do not bring reference books to the exam. They will only confuse those last minutes and be taken away from you when in the test room.
- Arrive somewhat ahead of time – If because of transportation schedules you must get there very early, bring a newspaper or magazine to take your mind off yourself while waiting.
- Locate the examination room – When you have found the proper room, you will be directed to the seat or part of the room where you will sit. Sometimes you are given a sheet of instructions to read while you are waiting. Do not fill out any forms until you are told to do so; just read them and be prepared.
- Relax and prepare to listen to the instructions
- If you have any physical problem that may keep you from doing your best, be sure to tell the test administrator. If you are sick or in poor health, you really cannot do your best on the exam. You can come back and take the test some other time.

VII. AT THE TEST

The day of the test is here and you have the test booklet in your hand. The temptation to get going is very strong. Caution! There is more to success than knowing the right answers. You must know how to identify your papers and understand variations in the type of short-answer question used in this particular examination. Follow these suggestions for maximum results from your efforts:

1) Cooperate with the monitor

The test administrator has a duty to create a situation in which you can be as much at ease as possible. He will give instructions, tell you when to begin, check to see that you are marking your answer sheet correctly, and so on. He is not there to guard you, although he will see that your competitors do not take unfair advantage. He wants to help you do your best.

2) Listen to all instructions

Don't jump the gun! Wait until you understand all directions. In most civil service tests you get more time than you need to answer the questions. So don't be in a hurry. Read each word of instructions until you clearly understand the meaning. Study the examples, listen to all announcements and follow directions. Ask questions if you do not understand what to do.

3) Identify your papers

Civil service exams are usually identified by number only. You will be assigned a number; you must not put your name on your test papers. Be sure to copy your number correctly. Since more than one exam may be given, copy your exact examination title.

4) Plan your time

Unless you are told that a test is a "speed" or "rate of work" test, speed itself is usually not important. Time enough to answer all the questions will be provided, but this does not mean that you have all day. An overall time limit has been set. Divide the total time (in minutes) by the number of questions to determine the approximate time you have for each question.

5) Do not linger over difficult questions

If you come across a difficult question, mark it with a paper clip (useful to have along) and come back to it when you have been through the booklet. One caution if you do this – be sure to skip a number on your answer sheet as well. Check often to be sure that you have not lost your place and that you are marking in the row numbered the same as the question you are answering.

6) Read the questions

Be sure you know what the question asks! Many capable people are unsuccessful because they failed to *read* the questions correctly.

7) Answer all questions

Unless you have been instructed that a penalty will be deducted for incorrect answers, it is better to guess than to omit a question.

8) Speed tests

It is often better NOT to guess on speed tests. It has been found that on timed tests people are tempted to spend the last few seconds before time is called in marking answers at random – without even reading them – in the hope of picking up a few extra points. To discourage this practice, the instructions may warn you that your score will be "corrected" for guessing. That is, a penalty will be applied. The incorrect answers will be deducted from the correct ones, or some other penalty formula will be used.

9) Review your answers

If you finish before time is called, go back to the questions you guessed or omitted to give them further thought. Review other answers if you have time.

10) Return your test materials

If you are ready to leave before others have finished or time is called, take ALL your materials to the monitor and leave quietly. Never take any test material with you. The monitor can discover whose papers are not complete, and taking a test booklet may be grounds for disqualification.

VIII. EXAMINATION TECHNIQUES

1) Read the general instructions carefully. These are usually printed on the first page of the exam booklet. As a rule, these instructions refer to the timing of the examination; the fact that you should not start work until the signal and must stop work at a signal, etc. If there are any *special* instructions, such as a choice of questions to be answered, make sure that you note this instruction carefully.

2) When you are ready to start work on the examination, that is as soon as the signal has been given, read the instructions to each question booklet, underline any key words or phrases, such as *least, best, outline, describe* and the like. In this way you will tend to answer as requested rather than discover on reviewing your paper that you *listed without describing*, that you selected the *worst* choice rather than the *best* choice, etc.

3) If the examination is of the objective or multiple-choice type – that is, each question will also give a series of possible answers: A, B, C or D, and you are called upon to select the best answer and write the letter next to that answer on your answer paper – it is advisable to start answering each question in turn. There may be anywhere from 50 to 100 such questions in the three or four hours allotted and you can see how much time would be taken if you read through all the questions before beginning to answer any. Furthermore, if you come across a question or group of questions which you know would be difficult to answer, it would undoubtedly affect your handling of all the other questions.

4) If the examination is of the essay type and contains but a few questions, it is a moot point as to whether you should read all the questions before starting to answer any one. Of course, if you are given a choice – say five out of seven and the like – then it is essential to read all the questions so you can eliminate the two that are most difficult. If, however, you are asked to answer all the questions, there may be danger in trying to answer the easiest one first because you may find that you will spend too much time on it. The best technique is to answer the first question, then proceed to the second, etc.

5) Time your answers. Before the exam begins, write down the time it started, then add the time allowed for the examination and write down the time it must be completed, then divide the time available somewhat as follows:
    - If 3-1/2 hours are allowed, that would be 210 minutes. If you have 80 objective-type questions, that would be an average of 2-1/2 minutes per question. Allow yourself no more than 2 minutes per question, or a total of 160 minutes, which will permit about 50 minutes to review.
    - If for the time allotment of 210 minutes there are 7 essay questions to answer, that would average about 30 minutes a question. Give yourself only 25 minutes per question so that you have about 35 minutes to review.

6) The most important instruction is to *read each question* and make sure you know what is wanted. The second most important instruction is to *time yourself properly* so that you answer every question. The third most important instruction is to *answer every question*. Guess if you have to but include something for each question. Remember that you will receive no credit for a blank and will probably receive some credit if you write something in answer to an essay question. If you guess a letter – say "B" for a multiple-choice question – you may have guessed right. If you leave a blank as an answer to a multiple-choice question, the examiners may respect your feelings but it will not add a point to your score. Some exams may penalize you for wrong answers, so in such cases *only*, you may not want to guess unless you have some basis for your answer.

7) Suggestions
    a. Objective-type questions
        1. Examine the question booklet for proper sequence of pages and questions
        2. Read all instructions carefully
        3. Skip any question which seems too difficult; return to it after all other questions have been answered
        4. Apportion your time properly; do not spend too much time on any single question or group of questions

5. Note and underline key words – *all, most, fewest, least, best, worst, same, opposite,* etc.
6. Pay particular attention to negatives
7. Note unusual option, e.g., unduly long, short, complex, different or similar in content to the body of the question
8. Observe the use of "hedging" words – *probably, may, most likely,* etc.
9. Make sure that your answer is put next to the same number as the question
10. Do not second-guess unless you have good reason to believe the second answer is definitely more correct
11. Cross out original answer if you decide another answer is more accurate; do not erase until you are ready to hand your paper in
12. Answer all questions; guess unless instructed otherwise
13. Leave time for review

b. Essay questions
1. Read each question carefully
2. Determine exactly what is wanted. Underline key words or phrases.
3. Decide on outline or paragraph answer
4. Include many different points and elements unless asked to develop any one or two points or elements
5. Show impartiality by giving pros and cons unless directed to select one side only
6. Make and write down any assumptions you find necessary to answer the questions
7. Watch your English, grammar, punctuation and choice of words
8. Time your answers; don't crowd material

8) Answering the essay question

Most essay questions can be answered by framing the specific response around several key words or ideas. Here are a few such key words or ideas:

M's: manpower, materials, methods, money, management
P's: purpose, program, policy, plan, procedure, practice, problems, pitfalls, personnel, public relations

a. Six basic steps in handling problems:
1. Preliminary plan and background development
2. Collect information, data and facts
3. Analyze and interpret information, data and facts
4. Analyze and develop solutions as well as make recommendations
5. Prepare report and sell recommendations
6. Install recommendations and follow up effectiveness

b. Pitfalls to avoid
1. *Taking things for granted* – A statement of the situation does not necessarily imply that each of the elements is necessarily true; for example, a complaint may be invalid and biased so that all that can be taken for granted is that a complaint has been registered

2. *Considering only one side of a situation* – Wherever possible, indicate several alternatives and then point out the reasons you selected the best one
3. *Failing to indicate follow up* – Whenever your answer indicates action on your part, make certain that you will take proper follow-up action to see how successful your recommendations, procedures or actions turn out to be
4. *Taking too long in answering any single question* – Remember to time your answers properly

IX. AFTER THE TEST

Scoring procedures differ in detail among civil service jurisdictions although the general principles are the same. Whether the papers are hand-scored or graded by machine we have described, they are nearly always graded by number. That is, the person who marks the paper knows only the number – never the name – of the applicant. Not until all the papers have been graded will they be matched with names. If other tests, such as training and experience or oral interview ratings have been given, scores will be combined. Different parts of the examination usually have different weights. For example, the written test might count 60 percent of the final grade, and a rating of training and experience 40 percent. In many jurisdictions, veterans will have a certain number of points added to their grades.

After the final grade has been determined, the names are placed in grade order and an eligible list is established. There are various methods for resolving ties between those who get the same final grade – probably the most common is to place first the name of the person whose application was received first. Job offers are made from the eligible list in the order the names appear on it. You will be notified of your grade and your rank as soon as all these computations have been made. This will be done as rapidly as possible.

People who are found to meet the requirements in the announcement are called "eligibles." Their names are put on a list of eligible candidates. An eligible's chances of getting a job depend on how high he stands on this list and how fast agencies are filling jobs from the list.

When a job is to be filled from a list of eligibles, the agency asks for the names of people on the list of eligibles for that job. When the civil service commission receives this request, it sends to the agency the names of the three people highest on this list. Or, if the job to be filled has specialized requirements, the office sends the agency the names of the top three persons who meet these requirements from the general list.

The appointing officer makes a choice from among the three people whose names were sent to him. If the selected person accepts the appointment, the names of the others are put back on the list to be considered for future openings.

That is the rule in hiring from all kinds of eligible lists, whether they are for typist, carpenter, chemist, or something else. For every vacancy, the appointing officer has his choice of any one of the top three eligibles on the list. This explains why the person whose name is on top of the list sometimes does not get an appointment when some of the persons lower on the list do. If the appointing officer chooses the second or third eligible, the No. 1 eligible does not get a job at once, but stays on the list until he is appointed or the list is terminated.

X. HOW TO PASS THE INTERVIEW TEST

The examination for which you applied requires an oral interview test. You have already taken the written test and you are now being called for the interview test – the final part of the formal examination.

You may think that it is not possible to prepare for an interview test and that there are no procedures to follow during an interview. Our purpose is to point out some things you can do in advance that will help you and some good rules to follow and pitfalls to avoid while you are being interviewed.

What is an interview supposed to test?

The written examination is designed to test the technical knowledge and competence of the candidate; the oral is designed to evaluate intangible qualities, not readily measured otherwise, and to establish a list showing the relative fitness of each candidate – as measured against his competitors – for the position sought. Scoring is not on the basis of "right" and "wrong," but on a sliding scale of values ranging from "not passable" to "outstanding." As a matter of fact, it is possible to achieve a relatively low score without a single "incorrect" answer because of evident weakness in the qualities being measured.

Occasionally, an examination may consist entirely of an oral test – either an individual or a group oral. In such cases, information is sought concerning the technical knowledges and abilities of the candidate, since there has been no written examination for this purpose. More commonly, however, an oral test is used to supplement a written examination.

Who conducts interviews?

The composition of oral boards varies among different jurisdictions. In nearly all, a representative of the personnel department serves as chairman. One of the members of the board may be a representative of the department in which the candidate would work. In some cases, "outside experts" are used, and, frequently, a businessman or some other representative of the general public is asked to serve. Labor and management or other special groups may be represented. The aim is to secure the services of experts in the appropriate field.

However the board is composed, it is a good idea (and not at all improper or unethical) to ascertain in advance of the interview who the members are and what groups they represent. When you are introduced to them, you will have some idea of their backgrounds and interests, and at least you will not stutter and stammer over their names.

What should be done before the interview?

While knowledge about the board members is useful and takes some of the surprise element out of the interview, there is other preparation which is more substantive. It *is* possible to prepare for an oral interview – in several ways:

1) Keep a copy of your application and review it carefully before the interview

This may be the only document before the oral board, and the starting point of the interview. Know what education and experience you have listed there, and the sequence and dates of all of it. Sometimes the board will ask you to review the highlights of your experience for them; you should not have to hem and haw doing it.

2) Study the class specification and the examination announcement

Usually, the oral board has one or both of these to guide them. The qualities, characteristics or knowledges required by the position sought are stated in these documents. They offer valuable clues as to the nature of the oral interview. For example, if the job involves supervisory responsibilities, the announcement will usually indicate that knowledge of modern supervisory methods and the qualifications of the candidate as a supervisor will be tested. If so, you can expect such questions, frequently in the form of a hypothetical situation which you are expected to solve. NEVER go into an oral without knowledge of the duties and responsibilities of the job you seek.

3) Think through each qualification required

Try to visualize the kind of questions you would ask if you were a board member. How well could you answer them? Try especially to appraise your own knowledge and background in each area, *measured against the job sought*, and identify any areas in which you are weak. Be critical and realistic – do not flatter yourself.

4) Do some general reading in areas in which you feel you may be weak

For example, if the job involves supervision and your past experience has NOT, some general reading in supervisory methods and practices, particularly in the field of human relations, might be useful. Do NOT study agency procedures or detailed manuals. The oral board will be testing your understanding and capacity, not your memory.

5) Get a good night's sleep and watch your general health and mental attitude

You will want a clear head at the interview. Take care of a cold or any other minor ailment, and of course, no hangovers.

What should be done on the day of the interview?

Now comes the day of the interview itself. Give yourself plenty of time to get there. Plan to arrive somewhat ahead of the scheduled time, particularly if your appointment is in the fore part of the day. If a previous candidate fails to appear, the board might be ready for you a bit early. By early afternoon an oral board is almost invariably behind schedule if there are many candidates, and you may have to wait. Take along a book or magazine to read, or your application to review, but leave any extraneous material in the waiting room when you go in for your interview. In any event, relax and compose yourself.

The matter of dress is important. The board is forming impressions about you – from your experience, your manners, your attitude, and your appearance. Give your personal appearance careful attention. Dress your best, but not your flashiest. Choose conservative, appropriate clothing, and be sure it is immaculate. This is a business interview, and your appearance should indicate that you regard it as such. Besides, being well groomed and properly dressed will help boost your confidence.

Sooner or later, someone will call your name and escort you into the interview room. *This is it.* From here on you are on your own. It is too late for any more preparation. But remember, you asked for this opportunity to prove your fitness, and you are here because your request was granted.

What happens when you go in?

The usual sequence of events will be as follows: The clerk (who is often the board stenographer) will introduce you to the chairman of the oral board, who will introduce you to the other members of the board. Acknowledge the introductions before you sit down. Do not be surprised if you find a microphone facing you or a stenotypist sitting by. Oral interviews are usually recorded in the event of an appeal or other review.

Usually the chairman of the board will open the interview by reviewing the highlights of your education and work experience from your application – primarily for the benefit of the other members of the board, as well as to get the material into the record. Do not interrupt or comment unless there is an error or significant misinterpretation; if that is the case, do not hesitate. But do not quibble about insignificant matters. Also, he will usually ask you some question about your education, experience or your present job – partly to get you to start talking and to establish the interviewing "rapport." He may start the actual questioning, or turn it over to one of the other members. Frequently, each member undertakes the questioning on a particular area, one in which he is perhaps most competent, so you can expect each member to participate in the examination. Because time is limited, you may also expect some rather abrupt switches in the direction the questioning takes, so do not be upset by it. Normally, a board member will not pursue a single line of questioning unless he discovers a particular strength or weakness.

After each member has participated, the chairman will usually ask whether any member has any further questions, then will ask you if you have anything you wish to add. Unless you are expecting this question, it may floor you. Worse, it may start you off on an extended, extemporaneous speech. The board is not usually seeking more information. The question is principally to offer you a last opportunity to present further qualifications or to indicate that you have nothing to add. So, if you feel that a significant qualification or characteristic has been overlooked, it is proper to point it out in a sentence or so. Do not compliment the board on the thoroughness of their examination – they have been sketchy, and you know it. If you wish, merely say, "No thank you, I have nothing further to add." This is a point where you can "talk yourself out" of a good impression or fail to present an important bit of information. Remember, *you close the interview yourself.*

The chairman will then say, "That is all, Mr. _____, thank you." Do not be startled; the interview is over, and quicker than you think. Thank him, gather your belongings and take your leave. Save your sigh of relief for the other side of the door.

How to put your best foot forward

Throughout this entire process, you may feel that the board individually and collectively is trying to pierce your defenses, seek out your hidden weaknesses and embarrass and confuse you. Actually, this is not true. They are obliged to make an appraisal of your qualifications for the job you are seeking, and they want to see you in your best light. Remember, they must interview all candidates and a non-cooperative candidate may become a failure in spite of their best efforts to bring out his qualifications. Here are 15 suggestions that will help you:

1) Be natural – Keep your attitude confident, not cocky

If you are not confident that you can do the job, do not expect the board to be. Do not apologize for your weaknesses, try to bring out your strong points. The board is interested in a positive, not negative, presentation. Cockiness will antagonize any board member and make him wonder if you are covering up a weakness by a false show of strength.

2) Get comfortable, but don't lounge or sprawl

Sit erectly but not stiffly. A careless posture may lead the board to conclude that you are careless in other things, or at least that you are not impressed by the importance of the occasion. Either conclusion is natural, even if incorrect. Do not fuss with your clothing, a pencil or an ashtray. Your hands may occasionally be useful to emphasize a point; do not let them become a point of distraction.

3) Do not wisecrack or make small talk

This is a serious situation, and your attitude should show that you consider it as such. Further, the time of the board is limited – they do not want to waste it, and neither should you.

4) Do not exaggerate your experience or abilities
In the first place, from information in the application or other interviews and sources, the board may know more about you than you think. Secondly, you probably will not get away with it. An experienced board is rather adept at spotting such a situation, so do not take the chance.

5) If you know a board member, do not make a point of it, yet do not hide it
Certainly you are not fooling him, and probably not the other members of the board. Do not try to take advantage of your acquaintanceship – it will probably do you little good.

6) Do not dominate the interview
Let the board do that. They will give you the clues – do not assume that you have to do all the talking. Realize that the board has a number of questions to ask you, and do not try to take up all the interview time by showing off your extensive knowledge of the answer to the first one.

7) Be attentive
You only have 20 minutes or so, and you should keep your attention at its sharpest throughout. When a member is addressing a problem or question to you, give him your undivided attention. Address your reply principally to him, but do not exclude the other board members.

8) Do not interrupt
A board member may be stating a problem for you to analyze. He will ask you a question when the time comes. Let him state the problem, and wait for the question.

9) Make sure you understand the question
Do not try to answer until you are sure what the question is. If it is not clear, restate it in your own words or ask the board member to clarify it for you. However, do not haggle about minor elements.

10) Reply promptly but not hastily
A common entry on oral board rating sheets is "candidate responded readily," or "candidate hesitated in replies." Respond as promptly and quickly as you can, but do not jump to a hasty, ill-considered answer.

11) Do not be peremptory in your answers
A brief answer is proper – but do not fire your answer back. That is a losing game from your point of view. The board member can probably ask questions much faster than you can answer them.

12) Do not try to create the answer you think the board member wants
He is interested in what kind of mind you have and how it works – not in playing games. Furthermore, he can usually spot this practice and will actually grade you down on it.

13) Do not switch sides in your reply merely to agree with a board member
Frequently, a member will take a contrary position merely to draw you out and to see if you are willing and able to defend your point of view. Do not start a debate, yet do not surrender a good position. If a position is worth taking, it is worth defending.

14) Do not be afraid to admit an error in judgment if you are shown to be wrong
The board knows that you are forced to reply without any opportunity for careful consideration. Your answer may be demonstrably wrong. If so, admit it and get on with the interview.

15) Do not dwell at length on your present job
The opening question may relate to your present assignment. Answer the question but do not go into an extended discussion. You are being examined for a *new* job, not your present one. As a matter of fact, try to phrase ALL your answers in terms of the job for which you are being examined.

Basis of Rating
Probably you will forget most of these "do's" and "don'ts" when you walk into the oral interview room. Even remembering them all will not ensure you a passing grade. Perhaps you did not have the qualifications in the first place. But remembering them will help you to put your best foot forward, without treading on the toes of the board members.

Rumor and popular opinion to the contrary notwithstanding, an oral board wants you to make the best appearance possible. They know you are under pressure – but they also want to see how you respond to it as a guide to what your reaction would be under the pressures of the job you seek. They will be influenced by the degree of poise you display, the personal traits you show and the manner in which you respond.

ABOUT THIS BOOK

This book contains tests divided into Examination Sections. Go through each test, answering every question in the margin. We have also attached a sample answer sheet at the back of the book that can be removed and used. At the end of each test look at the answer key and check your answers. On the ones you got wrong, look at the right answer choice and learn. Do not fill in the answers first. Do not memorize the questions and answers, but understand the answer and principles involved. On your test, the questions will likely be different from the samples. Questions are changed and new ones added. If you understand these past questions you should have success with any changes that arise. Tests may consist of several types of questions. We have additional books on each subject should more study be advisable or necessary for you. Finally, the more you study, the better prepared you will be. This book is intended to be the last thing you study before you walk into the examination room. Prior study of relevant texts is also recommended. NLC publishes some of these in our Fundamental Series. Knowledge and good sense are important factors in passing your exam. Good luck also helps. So now study this Passbook, absorb the material contained within and take that knowledge into the examination. Then do your best to pass that exam.

EXAMINATION SECTION

EXAMINATION SECTION
TEST 1

DIRECTIONS: Each question or incomplete statement is followed by several suggested answers or completions. Select the one that BEST answers the question or completes the statement. *PRINT THE LETTER OF THE CORRECT ANSWER IN THE SPACE AT THE RIGHT.*

1. There are a considerable number of forms and reports to be submitted on schedule by a building custodian.
   The ADVISABLE method of accomplishing this duty is to

   A. fill out the reports at odd times during the days when you have free time
   B. schedule a definite period of the work week for completing these forms and reports
   C. assign your foreman or cleaner to handle all these forms for you and to have them available on time
   D. classify or group the forms and reports and fill out only one of each group and refer the other forms or reports to the ones completed

   1._____

2. In enforcing compliance with safety regulations, you should take the attitude that they must be complied with because

   A. every accident can be prevented
   B. safety regulations are based on reason and experience with the best methods of accident prevention
   C. compliance with safety regulations will make other safety efforts unnecessary
   D. they are the law, and law enforcement is an end in itself

   2._____

3. The use of trisodium phosphate in cleaning marble should be avoided because

   A. it discolors the surface of the marble
   B. the salt crystals get in the pores, expand, and crack the marble
   C. it pits the glazed surface and bleaches the marble
   D. it builds up a slick surface on the marble

   3._____

4. The use of a concentrated cleaning solution on painted or varnished woodwork

   A. results in burning the pigments of paint or varnish, causing dull, streaky surfaces
   B. cuts down on time and energy in maintaining clean, unblemished surfaces
   C. insures spotless, clean, bright surfaces
   D. is detrimental to the health of the cleaners

   4._____

5. A building custodian will make the BEST impression on the office staff if he

   A. impresses them with the importance of his job
   B. says little and is cold and distant
   C. is easy-going and good-natured
   D. is courteous and performs his duties with as little delay as possible

   5._____

6. Domestic hot water storage reservoirs should be thoroughly cleaned once

   A. a week   B. a month
   C. a year   D. every two years

   6._____

1

7. A *pH* value of 4 would indicate a(n)

   A. acid solution
   B. neutral solution
   C. alkaline solution
   D. low pressure heating system

8. When the diaphragm or bellows of a thermostatic radiator trap is found to be dirty, it is USUALLY cleaned with

   A. turpentine
   B. carbon tetrachloride
   C. kerosene
   D. mild soap and water

9. The CHIEF purpose of a plumbing trap is to

   A. permit air to enter the sewer
   B. prevent the entrance of sewer gas into the building
   C. break the shock of the water draining off
   D. siphon off the waste water

10. The safety device on the gas pilot flame of a gas-fired apparatus should operate on pilot flame failure to

    A. bypass the main gas supply directly to the flue
    B. switch over to auxiliary bottled gas pilot flame
    C. shut off the gas supply
    D. introduce sufficient excess air to keep the furnace below the lower explosive limit

11. When instructing employees in regard to their duties in case of fire, a supervisor should

    A. tell employees to take no action until the fire department equipment has arrived
    B. tell all employees to go to the scene of the fire
    C. assign each employee specific duties
    D. tell employees to extinguish the fire before calling the supervisor or the fire department

12. The PRINCIPAL value of a good report is that it

    A. is always available for reference
    B. impresses department heads with the need for immediate action
    C. reflects upon the writer of the report
    D. expedites official business

13. The quality of work performed by personnel engaged in building cleaning is BEST evaluated by

    A. studying building cleaning expenditures
    B. studying time records of personnel
    C. analyzing complaints by building occupants
    D. inspecting the building periodically

14. Of the following, a building custodian need NOT be kept informed on

    A. departmental management policies
    B. terms of union contracts covering his subordinates
    C. developments of current interest in custodial operations
    D. current rate of interest on municipal bonds

15. The BEST way to make work assignments to persons required to clean a multi-story building is to

    A. allow the persons to pick their room or area assignments out of a hat
    B. make specific room or area assignments to each person separately
    C. rotate room and area assignments daily according to a chart posted on the bulletin board
    D. each week let a different member of the group make the room or area assignment

16. One important use of accident reports is to provide information that may be used to reduce the possibility of similar accidents.
    The MOST valuable entry on the report for this purpose is the

    A. name of the victim
    B. injury sustained by the victim
    C. cause of the accident
    D. location of the accident

17. Suppose that an emergency has arisen which requires you to cancel some of the jobs scheduled for that day.
    Of the following jobs, the one that can be eliminated for that day with LEAST effect on the proper operation and maintenance of the building is

    A. mopping and cleaning toilet rooms
    B. checking public stairs and corridors for hazards
    C. improving the location of supplies in the storeroom
    D. replacing broken window panes in offices

18. Of the following, a building custodian's attitude toward grievances should be to

    A. pay little attention to little grievances
    B. be very alert to grievances and make adjustments in existing conditions to appease all of them
    C. know the most frequent causes of grievances and strive to prevent them from arising
    D. maintain rigid discipline of a nature that *smoothes out* all grievances

19. A heavy snowfall must be removed from the sidewalks around the building. You, as building custodian, have assigned two men to shovel snow from the walks. After an interval, you check and find they are bickering as to how much each is shoveling, and no snow is being removed.
    In this situation, you should

    A. stand with them to supervise the snow removal and to be sure the work is divided evenly
    B. assign two other men to snow removal and send the original two back to their usual chores
    C. put the man with seniority in full charge of the other man
    D. separate the men by sending them to opposite ends of the walks to shovel alone, with a warning that you will be checking on their progress at short intervals

20. Of the following, safety on the job is BEST assured by

    A. keeping alert
    B. following every rule
    C. working very slowly
    D. never working alone

20.____

KEY (CORRECT ANSWERS)

1.	B	11.	C
2.	B	12.	D
3.	B	13.	D
4.	A	14.	D
5.	D	15.	B
6.	C	16.	C
7.	A	17.	C
8.	C	18.	C
9.	B	19.	D
10.	C	20.	A

TEST 2

DIRECTIONS: Each question or incomplete statement is followed by several suggested answers or completions. Select the one that BEST answers the question or completes the statement. *PRINT THE LETTER OF THE CORRECT ANSWER IN THE SPACE AT THE RIGHT.*

1. A foam-type fire extinguisher extinguishes fires by   1.____

    A. cooling *only*
    B. drenching *only*
    C. smothering *only*
    D. cooling and smothering

2. The extinguishing agent in a soda-acid fire extinguisher is   2.____

    A. carbon dioxide
    B. water
    C. carbon tetrachloride
    D. calcium chloride solution

3. The PROPER extinguisher to use on an electrical fire in an operating electric motor is   3.____

    A. foam
    B. carbon dioxide
    C. soda and acid
    D. water

4. When an extension ladder is in place and ready to be used, the rope used to extend the ladder should be   4.____

    A. left hanging free out of the way of the climber's feet
    B. used to raise and lower tools to the man on the ladder
    C. used as a means of steadying the climber
    D. tied securely around a lower rung

5. The PRINCIPAL characteristic of panic locks or bolts on doors of places of public assembly is that they   5.____

    A. allow the doors to open outwardly with sufficient pressure on the bars of the lock
    B. allow the doors to open inwardly with sufficient pressure on the bars of the lock
    C. prevent the door from opening under impact load
    D. may be opened with any tumbler lock key

6. The MAIN purpose of periodic inspections and tests of electrical equipment is to   6.____

    A. encourage the men to take better care of the equipment
    B. make the men familiar with the equipment
    C. discover minor faults before they develop into major faults
    D. keep the men busy during otherwise slack periods

7. Standard, extra strong, and double extra strong welded steel pipe of a given size all have the SAME   7.____

    A. outside diameter
    B. inside diameter
    C. average diameter
    D. flow capacity for any given flow velocity

8. In reference to domestic gas piping,

   A. couplings with running threads are used to join pipes
   B. risers must have a drip leg and cap at bottom
   C. gasketed unions may be used in joining pipe
   D. composition disc globe valves are used to throttle the gas

9. Chewing gum should be removed from rubber, asphalt, or linoleum flooring with

   A. a putty knife
   B. steel wool
   C. gritty compounds
   D. a solvent

10. Which one of the following is the BEST procedure to follow when the linoleum floor of a meeting room containing movable furniture is to be mopped?

    A. The furniture should be moved by sliding it along the floor to prevent injury to the cleaners.
    B. The furniture should not be moved.
    C. The furniture should be moved by lifting it and carrying it to a clear spot to prevent damage to the linoleum.
    D. Very little water should be used in order to prevent the legs of the furniture from getting wet.

11. Asphalt tile flooring that has been subjected to oily compounds

    A. may last indefinitely
    B. must be removed and replaced with new asphalt tile immediately
    C. may be restored to hardness and lustre by several moppings with hot water and several applications of water wax
    D. must be restored to original condition by several moppings with kerosene

12. The use of alcohol in water for washing windows is NOT recommended because it

    A. is a hazard to the cleaner in that he may be affected by the fumes
    B. will damage the paint around the edges of the glass
    C. pits the surface of the glass
    D. destroys the bristles of the brush applying the solution to the pane

13. Of the following, the BEST material to use for removing grass stains on marble or wood is

    A. oxalic acid
    B. chloride of lime
    C. sodium silicate
    D. sodium hypochlorite

14. Shades or Venetian blinds are PREFERABLY cleaned with a

    A. feather duster
    B. counter brush
    C. damp sponge
    D. vacuum cleaner

15. Asphalt tile floors are PREFERABLY polished with

    A. water emulsion wax
    B. wax in solution with benzol
    C. a high fatty acid soap
    D. sodium metaphosphate

16. Washing soda is used to   16._____

   A. eliminate the need for rinse mopping or wiping
   B. make the cleaning compound abrasive
   C. decrease the wetting power of water
   D. increase the wetting power of water

17. Varnish or lacquer may be used as a sealer on floors finished with   17._____

   A. asphalt tiles
   B. linoleum
   C. rubber tiles
   D. cork tiles

18. A long-handled deck scrub brush is MOST effective when scrubbing   18._____

   A. large open areas
   B. stair treads
   C. small flat areas
   D. long corridors

19. The BEST method for preventing the infestation of a building by rats is to   19._____

   A. use cats
   B. use rat traps
   C. eliminate rat harborages in the building
   D. use poisoned bait

20. The one of the following foodstuffs which, if allowed to remain on ordinary asphalt tile,   20._____
    will MOST likely be most injurious to it is

   A. milk
   B. maple syrup
   C. ketchup
   D. salad oil

KEY (CORRECT ANSWERS)

1.	D	11.	C
2.	B	12.	B
3.	B	13.	D
4.	D	14.	D
5.	A	15.	A
6.	C	16.	D
7.	A	17.	D
8.	B	18.	C
9.	A	19.	C
10.	C	20.	D

TEST 3

DIRECTIONS: Each question or incomplete statement is followed by several suggested answers or completions. Select the one that BEST answers the question or completes the statement. *PRINT THE LETTER OF THE CORRECT ANSWER IN THE SPACE AT THE RIGHT.*

1. Employees engaged in cleaning operations who are issued rubber gloves to protect their hands against caustic solutions should be warned that   1.____

   A. such solution allowed to spill over the glove top into the space between the glove and the hand may damage the skin of the hand
   B. rubber gloves have a very short life in contact with caustic solutions
   C. harmful gases can penetrate the rubber and harm even dry hands
   D. contact of the hands with glove-type rubber for over an hour is harmful

2. Pyrethrins are used as   2.____

   A. insecticides   B. germicides
   C. waxes   D. detergents

3. Water hammer is   3.____

   A. a special hammer used to remove scale from a radiator
   B. caused by water in steam lines
   C. caused by excessive boiler pressure
   D. caused by low water level in the boiler

4. Which of the following is USUALLY used in the construction of a steam pressure gauge?   4.____

   A. Perfect circle tube   B. Venturi tube
   C. Bourdon tube   D. Elastic linkage

5. Usually when a large room is gradually filled with people, the room temperature   5.____

   A. and humidity both decrease
   B. increases and the humidity decreases
   C. and humidity increase
   D. decreases and humidity increases

6. A foot valve at the intake end of the suction line of a pump serves MAINLY to   6.____

   A. maintain pump prime
   B. filter out large particles in the fluid
   C. increase the maximum suction lift of the pump
   D. increase pump flow rate

7. A pressure gauge attached to a standpipe system shows a pressure of 36 pounds per sq. in.   7.____
   The head of water, in feet, above the gauge is MOST NEARLY

   A. 24   B. 36   C. 60   D. 83

8. Of the following, the term *vapor barrier* would MOST likely be associated with

   A. electric service installation
   B. insulation materials
   C. fuel oil tank installation
   D. domestic gas piping

9. Pitot tubes are used to

   A. test feed water for impurities
   B. measure air or gas flow in a duct
   C. prevent overheating of elements of a steam gauge
   D. control the ignition system of an oil burner

10. In warm air heating and in ventilating systems, laboratories and kitchens should NOT be equipped with return ducts in order to

    A. keep air velocities in other returns as high as possible
    B. reduce fire hazards
    C. reduce the possibility of circulating odors through the system
    D. keep the temperature high in these rooms

11. One square foot of equivalent direct steam radiation (EDR) is equivalent to a heat emission of _____ BTU per _____.

    A. 150; hour
    B. 240; minute
    C. 150; minute
    D. 240; hour

12. Of the following, the one which is LEAST likely to cause continuous vibration of an operating motor is

    A. a faulty starting circuit
    B. excessive belt tension
    C. the misalignment of motor and driven equipment
    D. loose bearings

13. The function of a steam trap is to

    A. remove sediment and dirt from steam
    B. remove air and non-condensible gases from steam
    C. relieve excessive steam pressure to the atmosphere
    D. remove condensate from a pipe or an apparatus

14. The temperature at which air is just saturated with the moisture present in it is called its

    A. relative humidity
    B. absolute humidity
    C. humid temperature
    D. dew point

15. If scale forms on the seat of a float-operated boiler feed water regulator, the MOST likely result is

    A. internal corrosion of the boiler shell
    B. insufficient supply of water to the boiler
    C. flooding of the boiler
    D. shutting down of the oil burner by the low water cut-out

16. The compound gauge in the oil suction line shows a high vacuum. This is USUALLY an indication of

    A. a dirty oil strainer
    B. low oil level in the fuel oil storage tank
    C. a leak in the fuel oil preheater
    D. an obstruction in the fuel oil preheater

17. Of the following, the information which is LEAST important on a boiler room log sheet is the

    A. stack temperature readings
    B. CO_2 readings
    C. number of boilers in operation
    D. boiler room humidity

18. Pitting and corrosion of the water side of the boiler heating surfaces is due MAINLY to the boiler water containing dissolved

    A. oxygen
    B. hydrogen
    C. soda-ash
    D. sodium sulphite

19. The combustion efficiency of a boiler can be determined with a CO_2

    A. flue gas temperature
    B. boiler room humidity
    C. outside air temperature
    D. under fire draft

20. The try-cocks of steam boilers are used to

    A. find the height of water in the boiler
    B. test steam pressure in the boiler
    C. empty the boiler of water
    D. act as safety valves

KEY (CORRECT ANSWERS)

1.	A	11.	D
2.	A	12.	A
3.	B	13.	D
4.	C	14.	D
5.	C	15.	C
6.	A	16.	A
7.	D	17.	D
8.	B	18.	A
9.	B	19.	A
10.	C	20.	A

TEST 4

DIRECTIONS: Each question or incomplete statement is followed by several suggested answers or completions. Select the one that BEST answers the question or completes the statement. *PRINT THE LETTER OF THE CORRECT ANSWER IN THE SPACE AT THE RIGHT.*

1. The reason for sweating inside a refrigerator cabinet is 1._____

   A. high percent running time of compressor unit
   B. high cabinet air temperature
   C. defective expansion valve
   D. a poor door seal

2. Of the following ingredients, the ones to be mixed with water to *point-up* the brickwork of a building are: 1 part cement, 2._____

   A. 2 parts sand, 3 parts gravel
   B. 3 parts sand, 4 parts gravel
   C. 3 parts sand
   D. 5 parts sand

3. Acid soils can BEST be neutralized by liberal applications of 3._____

   A. manure B. salt
   C. lime D. powdered-basalt

4. Summer blooming flower bulbs should be stored in a _____ place. 4._____

   A. warm, dry B. warm, moist
   C. cool, moist D. cool, dry

5. A certain 31-day month had an average temperature of 45 Fahrenheit. The number of degree days for this month is 5._____

   A. 31 B. 450 C. 620 D. 1395

6. While concrete is *curing*, it is MOST desirable to 6._____

   A. expose the concrete to sun and air as much as possible
   B. keep the concrete surface moist
   C. maintain a temperature of not more than 60°F
   D. maintain a temperature of at least 80°F

7. To join two lengths of pipe together in a solid straight run, the fitting to use is a 7._____

   A. coupling B. tee
   C. hickey D. shoulder nipple

8. New copper flashing that has been soldered should be 8._____

   A. muriatic acid B. plain water
   C. benzine D. washing soda or lye

9. The intercooler of a two-stage air compressor is connected to the compressor between the

   A. two stages
   B. filter and the first stage
   C. second stage and the receiver
   D. receiver and point of usage of the air

   9.____

10. Both terms *tank* and *close* apply USUALLY to

    A. electric generator couplings
    B. freon storage units
    C. pipe nipples
    D. ventilation plenum chambers

    10.____

11. The commercial fertilizer *5-10-5* refers to

    A. 5% nitrogen, 10% phosphoric acid, 5% potash
    B. 5% rotted manure, 10% calcium chloride, 5% bone meal
    C. 5% soda, 10% tobacco dust, 5% bone meal
    D. 5% tobacco dust, 10% rotted manure, 5% sulphur

    11.____

12. The slope or slant of a soil line is 1/4" per foot. If this drainage line is 50' long, the difference in elevation from one end to the other is, in feet, MOST NEARLY

    A. 0.55   B. 1.04   C. 2.08   D. 12.5

    12.____

13. Oil is used with sharpening stones when sharpening wood chisels in order to

    A. reduce the effort needed to move the blade over the stone
    B. maintain the oil temper of the steel used for the chisel
    C. flush off the small metal chips and clear the cutting edges of the abrasive grit
    D. reduce the temperature due to friction

    13.____

14. A maintenance man checking a refrigerator for a freon leak would use a

    A. soap and water solution
    B. halide torch
    C. glycerine solution
    D. linseed oil and whiting solution

    14.____

15. A basement floor area of 5000 square feet is under 9 inches of water.
    If this 9 inches of water is to be pumped out of the basement in one hour, the required capacity of the portable pump, in gallons per minute, is MOST NEARLY

    A. 63   B. 470   C. 1020   D. 2810

    15.____

16. A MAJOR advantage of keeping a perpetual inventory of supplies is that it

    A. gives a current record of the supplies available at all times
    B. reduces the work required to distribute supplies
    C. avoids the need for periodic physical inventories
    D. shows who is using excessive supplies

    16.____

17. Employees generally do NOT object to strict rules and regulations if they

    A. are enforced without bias or favor
    B. result in more material gain
    C. deal with relatively unimportant phases of the work
    D. affect the supervisors more than their subordinates

18. In order to have building employees willing to follow standardized cleaning and maintenance procedures, the supervisor MUST be prepared to

    A. work alongside the employees
    B. demonstrate the reasonableness of the procedures
    C. offer incentive pay for their use
    D. be adamant in opposing changes in the standardized procedures

19. Of the following, the MOST important step when accepting incoming shipments of standard items normally carried in stock is to check the items for

    A. electrical performance
    B. chemical composition
    C. quantity delivered
    D. mechanical performance

20. The orderly arrangement of supplies in storage USUALLY

    A. takes too much time to be worthwhile
    B. is important only in large warehouses
    C. is essential for stock selection and inventory purposes
    D. cannot be accomplished when package sizes vary

KEY (CORRECT ANSWERS)

1.	D	11.	A
2.	C	12.	B
3.	C	13.	C
4.	D	14.	B
5.	C	15.	B
6.	B	16.	A
7.	A	17.	A
8.	D	18.	B
9.	A	19.	C
10.	C	20.	C

EXAMINATION SECTION
TEST 1

DIRECTIONS: Each question or incomplete statement is followed by several suggested answers or completions. Select the one that BEST answers the question or completes the statement. *PRINT THE LETTER OF THE CORRECT ANSWER IN THE SPACE AT THE RIGHT.*

1. Of the following, the PREFERRED sequence of tasks to be followed in office cleaning is   1._____

   A. dust desks, empty ash trays and waste baskets, mop floor
   B. mop floor, dust desks, empty ash trays and waste baskets
   C. empty ash trays and waste baskets, dust desks, mop floor
   D. mop floor, empty ash trays and waste baskets, dust desks

2. When vacuum cleaning rugs, the suction tool should be pushed   2._____

   A. diagonally across the lay of the nap
   B. with the lay of the nap
   C. across the lay of the nap
   D. against the lay of the nap

3. The brownish discoloration that sometimes occurs in hot water circulating systems is USUALLY due to   3._____

   A. molds   B. algae   C. bacteria   D. rust

4. The type of valve that does NOT have a stuffing or packing gland is a _____ valve.   4._____

   A. globe   B. radiator   C. check   D. gate

5. Assuming that the hot and cold water demand of a fixture will be the same, then the normal size of the hot water pipe with respect to that of the cold water pipe should be   5._____

   A. the same
   C. one and one-half times as great
   B. twice as great
   D. one half as great

6. If the pitch of a horizontal steam line is 1/2 inch in 10 feet, one end of a 45-foot steam line is lower than the other end by, MOST NEARLY, _____ inches.   6._____

   A. 2   B. 2 1/4   C. 3   D. 3 1/2

7. A pump that removes 30 gallons of water per minute is pumping water from a cellar 30 feet x 50 feet covered with eight inches of water. One cubic foot of water equals 7.5 gallons of water.
   The number of minutes it will take to remove the eight inches of water from the cellar is, MOST NEARLY,   7._____

   A. 200   B. 225   C. 250   D. 275

8. Oil preheaters are used to   8._____

   A. economize on fuel oil
   C. improve the flow of oil
   B. reduce friction in the oil blower
   D. reduce oil volatility

15

9. The FIRST item which should be checked when a sump pit overflows because the automatic electric sump pump is not operating properly is the

    A. feedwater pressure
    B. ficat switch mechanism
    C. stat switch
    D. discharge line check valve

10. Chloride of lime should be used for the removal of

    A. alkali stains on wood
    B. grass stains on wood or marble
    C. indelible pencil and marking ink stains on concrete or terrazzo
    D. ink stains on wood

11. Of the following, the lack of a vapor barrier on the inside surface of a well-insulated wall may eventually cause, during the winter,

    A. plugging of weep holes
    B. peeling of exterior paint
    C. lower heat losses through the wall
    D. improvement in insulation performance by plugging air spaces with the insulation

12. When cold water pipes in a room *sweat*, it is USUALLY due to the

    A. surface of the pipes being below the dew point temperature of the room air
    B. specific humidity exceeding the relative humidity
    C. air in the room exceeding 100% relative humidity
    D. surface of the pipe being below the wet bulb temperature of the room air

13. The MAIN reason for applying floor finish to a floor surface is to

    A. protect against germs
    B. protect the floor surface
    C. increase traction
    D. waterproof the floor

14. The MAIN reason for preventing sewer gas from entering buildings through the plumbing system is because the gas

    A. is highly inflammable and explosive in nature and could result in a fire hazard
    B. has an eroding effect on plumbing fixtures and pipe lines
    C. is highly infectious and contagious in nature
    D. has a nuisance effect on occupants

15. The one of the following that is a concrete floor sealer is

    A. sodium silicate
    B. neatsfoot oil
    C. sodium hydroxide
    D. linseed oil

16. To help plants survive the shock of transplanting, in most cases, it is BEST to

    A. spray them with insecticide every day for a week
    B. cover the foliage with burlap for a day or two
    C. shade them from the sun for a week or two
    D. prune them every day for a week or two

3 (#1)

17. When cutting a branch off a tree, it is desirable to undercut because it will 17._____

   A. prevent the weight of the branch from tearing off bark and wood below the cut
   B. make the tree grow stronger and straighter
   C. let the saw work smoother and easier
   D. make it easier to cut up the limb

18. The *MAIN* reason for applying lime to soil is to control its 18._____

   A. aridity   B. fertilization
   C. acidity   D. porosity

19. The *GREATEST* danger to a tree from a large unprotected wound is that 19._____

   A. birds may build a nest in it
   B. the tree may bleed to death
   C. the wound may become infected
   D. it is open to the elements

20. The fertilizer that is used for the care of trees should have a high content of 20._____

   A. DDT   B. nitrogen   C. sulphur   D. carbon

21. The area of the plot plan shown below is _____ square feet. 21._____

   A. 25,300
   B. 26,700
   C. 28,100
   D. 30,500

22. The *BEST* of the following combinations of instruments to use in checking the combustion efficiency of a heating boiler is 22._____

   A. anemometer, stack thermometer, and orsat apparatus
   B. draft gage, psychrometer, and barometer
   C. draft gage, stack thermometer, and orsat apparatus
   D. draft gage, stack thermometer, and barometer

23. The one of the following that does NOT indicate low water in a steam boiler is the 23._____

   A. fusible plug   B. safety valve
   C. tri cocks   D. gauge glass

24. The increase in the stack temperature toward the end of the heating system above what it was at the beginning of the season is an indication that the 24._____

   A. radiators and convectors are air bound
   B. tubes and heating surfaces of the boiler are becoming insulated with soot
   C. furnace fire brick is failing
   D. heat content of the fuel is improving

25. Of the following, the one which is NOT a general class of oil burners is the _____ atomizing.

    A. water B. rotary cup C. mechanical D. air

26. Of the following, the one which should be between a boiler and its safety valve is

    A. a swing check valve of a size larger than that of the safety valve
    B. a butterfly valve located in the boiler-nozzle
    C. a gate valve of the same nominal size as that of the safety valve
    D. no valve of any type

27. The term *spinner cup* refers to

    A. screw-type stokers
    B. gun-type oil burners
    C. rotary-type oil burners
    D. chain grate stokers

28. A *gun-type* burner is often used on a

    A. pot-type oil burner
    B. low pressure gas boiler
    C. coal underfeed stoker boiler
    D. high pressure oil-fired boiler

29. Of the following, the action that should be taken as the FIRST step if a properly adjusted safety valve on a steam boiler *pops off* when in operation is

    A. open the-draft
    B. add more water to the boiler
    C. wire the valve shut
    D. reduce the draft

30. When the water gets below the safe level in an operating boiler, it is BEST to

    A. add new water up to the safe level and open up the fire so that the water will heat quickly
    B. check the fire and let the boiler cool down before new water is added
    C. add new water to the boiler immediately
    D. check the fire and empty the boiler

31. Vents on fuel oil storage tanks are used to

    A. fill the fuel tanks
    B. allow air to escape during filling
    C. check oil flash points
    D. make tank fuel soundings

32. Of the following, the MOST desirable way to remove carbon deposits from the atomizing cup of an oil burner is to

    A. apply a hot flame to the carbonized surfaces to burn off the carbon deposits
    B. use kerosene to loosen the deposits and wipe with a soft cloth
    C. wash the cup with a mild trisodium phosphate solution and dry with a cloth
    D. use a scraper, followed by light rubbing with emery cloth

33. Of the following, the MOST important precaution that should be taken when *cutting in* a boiler in a battery is to see that the

    A. water column is at least 1 inch below top row of tubes
    B. non-return valve is closed when the boiler pressure is rising
    C. safety valves function properly
    D. boiler pressure is about equal to header pressure

34. A condensate feedwater tank in a low pressure steam plant

    A. is hermetically sealed to prevent contamination of feed water
    B. contains a surface blow down line
    C. is vented to the atmosphere
    D. has a vacuum breaker exposed to the atmosphere

35. Of the following, the FIRST action to take in the event a low pressure steam boiler gauge glass breaks is to

    A. bank the fires
    B. close the water gauge glass cocks
    C. open the safety valve
    D. blow down the boiler

36. A *barometric damper* would be used in a boiler installation fired under draft conditions that are called

    A. induced   B. natural   C. regenerate   D. forced

37. The flue gas temperature, when firing oil, should be just high enough to evaporate any contained moisture in order to

    A. prevent an acid from forming and eroding the breeching
    B. decrease the amount of excess air needed
    C. prevent an air pollution condition
    D. lower the combustion efficiency of the boiler

38. A compound gauge in a boiler room

    A. measures pressures above and below atmospheric pressure
    B. indicates the degree of compounding in a steam engine
    C. shows the quantity of boiler treatment compound on hand
    D. measures steam and water pressure

39. In the combustion of the common fuels, the PRINCIPAL boiler heat loss is that due to the heat

    A. carried away by the moisture in the fuel
    B. lost by radiation
    C. carried away by the flue gases
    D. lost by incomplete combustion

40. Of the following, the CORRECT sequence of steps to use when removing a boiler from service in order to perform extensive repairs on it is

    A. discontinue firing, drain boiler, turn off valves, cool boiler
    B. discontinue firing, drain boiler, turn off valves
    C. turn off valves, drain boiler, discontinue firing, cool boiler
    D. discontinue firing, turn off valves, cool boiler, drain boiler

40. _____

KEY (CORRECT ANSWERS)

1. C	11. B	21. C	31. B
2. B	12. A	22. C	32. B
3. D	13. B	23. B	33. D
4. C	14. D	24. B	34. C
5. A	15. A	25. A	35. B
6. B	16. C	26. D	36. B
7. C	17. A	27. C	37. A
8. C	18. C	28. D	38. A
9. B	19. C	29. D	39. C
10. C	20. B	30. B	40. D

TEST 2

DIRECTIONS: Each question or incomplete statement is followed by several suggested answers or completions. Select the one that BEST answers the question or completes the statement. *PRINT THE LETTER OF THE CORRECT ANSWER IN THE SPACE AT THE RIGHT.*

1. With the same outdoor winter temperatures, the load on a heating boiler starting up is greater than the normal morning load *MAINLY* because of   1.____

   A. loss of heat escaping through the stack
   B. steam required to heat boiler water and piping to radiators
   C. viscosity of the fuel oil
   D. low outdoor temperatures

2. The *FIRST* operation when starting a boiler after it has been on bank overnight should be to   2.____

   A. blow down the boiler
   B. clean the furnace
   C. check the gate valves
   D. look at the water gauge and try the gauge cocks

3. *Cascading* of raw city water when filling a cleaned boiler should be avoided because it   3.____

   A. is harmful to the mud drum
   B. adds additional free oxygen in the boiler
   C. adds considerable time to the filling procedure
   D. will stress tube and sheet joints

4. The average temperature on a day in January was 24° F. The number of degree-days for that day was   4.____

   A. 12   B. 24   C. 41   D. 48

5. Under normal conditions during the growing season, lawns should receive a good saturation of water with a spray   5.____

   A. once a day   B. once a week
   C. once a month   D. twice a month

6. One of the important benefits to floors that wax does *NOT* provide is   6.____

   A. easier soil removal   B. improved stain resistance
   C. reduction in wear   D. resistance to fire

7. In the Ringelmann chart of smoke density, number 4 indicates   7.____

   A. the darkest smoke condition
   B. the lightest smoke condition
   C. smoke density of 80 per cent
   D. no smoke condition

8. Of the following, the estinguishing agent that should be used on fires in flammable liquids is

   A. steam B. water C. foam D. soda and acid

9. A soda-acid fire extinguisher is recommended for use on fires consisting of

   A. wood or paper
   B. fuel oil or gasoline
   C. electrical causes or fuel oil
   D. paint or turpentine

10. The CHIEF reason wooden ladders should NOT be painted is that the paint may

    A. hide defects
    B. mark up the walls
    C. make the ladder slippery
    D. damage the rungs

11. In accordance with the uniform method of identifying piping in public buildings, pipes carrying materials classified as being dangerous are colored

    A. blue
    B. red
    C. orange and yellow
    D. green and white

12. The MOST effective way to eliminate fire hazards in public buildings is to

    A. hold frequent fire drills
    B. have the fire department inspect the building annually
    C. promote constant self-inspection
    D. supply each building with ample fire fighting equipment

13. When a room is air conditioned in the summer, the windows should be

    A. opened at the top and bottom to improve circulation
    B. screened to keep out the dirt
    C. kept closed
    D. opened at the top only to let hot air escape

14. In order to clean an office with 20,000 sq. ft. of space in four hours, using a standard of 900 sq. ft. per hour, the number of cleaners you should assign to do the job is MOST NEARLY

    A. 4 B. 6 C. 8 D. 10

15. The area of a floor 35' wide and 45' long is, in square yards, MOST NEARLY

    A. 175 B. 262 C. 525 D. 1575

16. A pyrometer is an instrument used for measuring

    A. condensation and humidity
    B. high temperatures
    C. noise pollution
    D. water flow

17. It is usually desirable to assign the cleaning of an office to one employee only because   17._____

    A. the amount of time wasted through talking is decreased
    B. an employee working alone, by himself, is more efficient
    C. there is no question who is responsible for the work done
    D. working alone reduces the rate and severity of accidents

18. Of each dollar spent on the cleaning of public buildings, the amount spent on cleaning supplies is usually not more than _____ cents.   18._____

    A. 5   B. 35   C. 55   D. 75

19. Of the following solutions, the one MOST often used in washing exterior glass is _____ water and a small quantity of _____.   19._____

    A. cold; turpentine   B. cold; ammonia
    C. cold; glass wax   D. warm; soft soap

20. Rust stains in wash basins can BEST be prevented by   20._____

    A. applying wax film to the rusty surface
    B. replacing leaking faucet washers
    C. adding rust inhibitor to the domestic cold water storage tank
    D. sand papering the rusty surfaces

21. Of the following, the one which is likely to be MOST harmful to asphalt tile is   21._____

    A. coffee   B. ketchup   C. salad oil   D. vinegar

22. Of the following, when sweeping a corridor with a floor brush, the cleaner should   22._____

    A. lean on the brush and walk the length of the corridor
    B. give the brush a slight jerk after each stroke to free it of loose dirt
    C. make certain there is no overlap on sweeping strokes
    D. use moderately long pull strokes

23. Time standards for cleaning are of value ONLY if   23._____

    A. a bonus is promised if the time standards are beaten
    B. the cleaners determine the methods and procedures to be used
    C. accompanied by a completely detailed description of the methods to be used
    D. a schematic diagram of the area is made available to the cleaners

24. Of the following, the one which is the LEAST important factor in deciding that additional training is necessary for the men you supervise is that   24._____

    A. the quality of work is below standard
    B. supplies are being wasted
    C. too much time is required to do specific jobs
    D. the absentee rate has declined

25. To promote proper safety practices in the operation of power tools and equipment, you should emphasize in meetings with the staff that   25._____

    A. every accident can be prevented through proper safety regulations
    B. proper safety practices will probably make future safety meetings unnecessary

C. when safety rules are followed, tools and equipment will work better
D. safety rules are based on past experience with the best methods of preventing accidents

26. A good practical method to use in determining whether an employee is doing his job properly is to

   A. assume that if he asks no questions, he knows the work
   B. question him directly on details of the job
   C. inspect and follow up the work which is assigned to him
   D. ask other employees how this employee is making out

27. If an employee continually asks how he should do his work, you should

   A. dismiss him immediately
   B. pretend you do not hear him unless he persists
   C. explain the work carefully but encourage him to use his own judgment
   D. tell him not to ask so many questions

28. You have instructed an employee to wet-mop a certain area. To be sure that the employee understands the instructions you have given him, you should

   A. ask him to repeat the instructions to you
   B. check with him after he has done the job
   C. watch him while he is doing the job
   D. repeat the instructions to the employee

29. One of your men disagrees with your evaluation of his work.
Of the following, the BEST way to handle this situation would be to

   A. explain that you are in a better position to evaluate his work than he is
   B. tell him that since other men are satisfied with your evaluation, he should accept their opinions
   C. explain the basis of your evaluation and discuss it with him
   D. refuse to discuss his complaint in order to maintain discipline

30. Of the following, the one which is NOT a quality of leadership desirable in a supervisor is

   A. intelligence   B. integrity
   C. forcefulness   D. partiality

31. Of the following, the one which LEAST characterizes the *grapevine* is that it

   A. consists of a tremendous amount of rumor, conjecture, information, advice, prediction, and even orders
   B. seems to rise spontaneously, is largely anonymous, spreads rapidly, and changes in unpredictable directions
   C. can be eliminated without any great effort
   D. commonly fills the gaps left by the regular organizational channels of communication

32. Of the following, the one which is NOT a purpose of a cleaning job breakdown is to

   A. eliminate unnecessary steps
   B. determine the type of floor wax to use

C. rearrange the sequence of operations to save time
D. combine steps or actions where practicable

33. Of the following, the PRINCIPAL function of a supervisor is to

    A. train and instruct his subordinates in the proper methods of doing their work
    B. eliminate all accidents
    C. prepare reports on his activities to his supervisor
    D. prepare a thorough job methods analysis

34. The BEST method of making cleaning assignments in a large building is by means of

    A. daily rotation   B. specific assignment
    C. individual choice   D. chronological order

35. When one of your new cleaning employees is making little progress after the usual training period with one of your experienced men, you should

    A. recommend to your superior that he should be discharged
    B. tell your superior he is not interested in the job
    C. determine the reason for the poor results
    D. discontinue all training

36. For a supervisor to have his cleaning employees willing to follow standardized cleaning procedures, he must be prepared to

    A. associate with his employees
    B. show that the procedures are reasonable
    C. give extra time off
    D. set up a penalty system

37. One of the employees you supervise has broken the rule against keeping liquor in his locker.
    You should

    A. make believe it never happened and forget the incident
    B. explain the rule to him and that a repetition may result in disciplinary action
    C. suspend him immediately
    D. fire him immediately

38. The BEST action for you to take on receiving complaints of poor illumination in one of the offices is to

    A. wait until you have several complaints of this kind
    B. tell the complainant nothing can be done
    C. request that additional ceiling lights be installed
    D. check the office for the cause of poor illumination

39. The MAIN purpose of periodic inspections and tests of mechanical equipment is to

    A. keep the men busy during otherwise slack periods
    B. discover minor faults before they develop into major faults
    C. make the men familiar with the equipment
    D. encourage the men to take better care of the equipment

40. Assume that one of your employees has been slightly injured while doing a cleaning job. After the employee has been cared for, you should NEXT

    A. investigate the cause of the accident
    B. notify the union
    C. charge the employee with recklessness
    D. transfer the employee

KEY (CORRECT ANSWERS)

1. B	11. C	21. C	31. C
2. D	12. C	22. B	32. B
3. B	13. C	23. C	33. A
4. C	14. B	24. D	34. B
5. B	15. A	25. D	35. C
6. D	16. B	26. C	36. B
7. C	17. C	27. C	37. B
8. C	18. A	28. A	38. D
9. A	19. B	29. C	39. B
10. A	20. B	30. D	40. A

EXAMINATION SECTION
TEST 1

DIRECTIONS: Each question or incomplete statement is followed by several suggested answers or completions. Select the one that BEST answers the question or completes the statement. *PRINT THE LETTER OF THE CORRECT ANSWER IN THE SPACE AT THE RIGHT.*

1. The KEY figure in any custodial safety program is the 1.____
   A. custodian   B. cleaner   C. mayor   D. commissioner

2. A custodian must inspect or have a maintenance man inspect every window cleaner's safety belt AT LEAST 2.____
   A. each time the windows are washed
   B. once a month
   C. once a year
   D. once every second year

3. A custodian's written instruction to his staff on the subject of security in public buildings should include instructions to 3.____
   A. exclude the public at all times
   B. admit the public at all times
   C. admit the public only if they are neat and well-dressed
   D. admit the public during specified hours

4. A custodian in charge of a building who is normally on duty during the daytime hours in a building which is cleaned at night should 4.____
   A. never make night inspections since he is not responsible for the cleanliness of the building
   B. make night inspections at least once a year
   C. never make night inspections because the cleaners will think he is spying on them
   D. make night inspections at least twice a month

5. The employee MOST likely to find the nests and runways in a building of roaches and vermin is a 5.____
   A. maintenance man   B. building custodian
   C. night cleaner   D. stationary fireman

6. When mopping, the pails containing the cleaning solutions should be 6.____
   A. slid along the floor to avoid injury due to lifting
   B. kept off the floor, preferably on a rolling platform
   C. shifted from place to place using a mop
   D. equipped with a spigot for applying the mopping solution

7. Of the following, the item that is considered a concrete floor sealer is
   A. water wax
   B. sodium hypochlorite
   C. sodium silicate
   D. linseed oil

8. A material COMMONLY used in detergent is
   A. rock salt
   B. Glauber's salt
   C. tri-sodium phosphate
   D. monosodium glutamate

9. A disinfectant material is one that will
   A. kill germs
   B. dissolve soil and stop odors
   C. give a clean odor and cover a disagreeable odor
   D. prevent soil buildup

10. When scrubbing a wooden floor, it is ADVISABLE to
    A. flood the surface with the cleaning solution in order to float the soil out of all crevices
    B. hose off the loosened soil before starting the scrubbing operation
    C. pick up the used solution as soon as possible
    D. mix a mild acid with the cleaning solution in order to clean the surface quickly

11. Before starting a wall washing operation, it is BEST to
    A. check the temperature of the water
    B. soak the sponge to be used
    C. check the pH of the mixed cleaning solution
    D. dust the wall to be washed

12. Of the following, the MOST nearly correct statement regarding the economical operation of the heating system in a building is that
    A. the heat should always be shut down at 4 P.M. and turned on at 8 A.M.
    B. the heat should be shut down only over the weekend
    C. it is best to keep the heat on at all times so that the number of complaints are kept to a minimum
    D. the times at which the heat is shut down and turned on should be varied depending on the prevailing outdoor temperature

13. A floor made of marble or granite chis imbedded in cement is USUALLY called
    A. terrazzo   B. linoleum   C. palmetto   D. parquet

14. In a 4-wire, 3-phase electrical supply system, the voltage between one phase and ground used for the lighting is MOST NEARLY
    A. 440   B. 230   C. 208   D. 115

15. Of the following, the one that takes the place of a fuse in an electrical circuit is a
    A. transformer
    B. circuit breaker
    C. condenser
    D. knife switch

16. Gas bills are USUALLY computed on the basis of
    A. cubic feet   B. gallons   C. pounds   D. kilowatts

17. An operating oil-fired steam boiler explosion may sometimes be caused by
    A. carrying too high a water level in the boiler
    B. inadequate purging of combustion chamber between fires
    C. overfiring the boiler
    D. carrying too high an oil temperature

18. The one of the following commercial sizes of anthracite which is the LARGEST in size is
    A. stove   B. chestnut   C. pea   D. rice

19. Assume that six windows of a public building facing one street have been consistently broken by boys playing ball after hours and over weekends.
    The BEST solution to this problem is to
    A. post a no ball playing sign on the wall
    B. erect protective screening outside the six windows
    C. post a guard on weekend patrol duty
    D. request special weekend police protection for the property

20. The BEST method or tool to use for cleaning dust from an unplastered cinder-block wall is
    A. a Tampico brush with stock cleaning solution
    B. a vacuum cleaner
    C. water under pressure from hose and nozzle
    D. a feather duster

21. Of the following, the LARGEST individual item of expense in operating a public building is generally the cost of
    A. cleaning   B. heating fuel
    C. electricity   D. elevator service

22. The CHIEF purpose for changing the handle of a floor brush from one side of the brush block to the other side is to
    A. allow the janitor to change hands
    B. make both sides of the brush equally dirty
    C. give both sides of the brush equal wear
    D. change the angle of sweeping

23. Of the following, the weight of mop MOST likely used in the nightly mopping of corridors, halls, or lobbies is _____ ounce.
    A. 8   B. 16   C. 24   D. 50

24. After sweeping assignment is completed, floor brushes should be stored
    A. in a pan of water
    B. by hanging the brushes on pegs or nails
    C. by piling the brushes on each other carefully
    D. in a normal sweeping position, bristles resting on the floor

25. Nylon-treated scrubbing discs
    A. require more water than scrubbing brushes
    B. require more detergent solution than scrubbing brushes
    C. must be used with cold water only
    D. are generally more effective than steel wool pads

26. Of the following, the BEST material to use to clean exterior bronze is
    A. pumice   B. paste wax
    C. wire wheel on portable buffer   D. lemon oil polish

27. The use of trisodium phosphate in cleaning polished marble should be AVOIDED because it
    A. may cause spalling
    B. discolors the surface of the marble
    C. builds up a slick surface on the marble
    D. pits the glazed surface and bleaches the marble

28. The floor area, in square feet, on which a properly treated dustless sweeping cloth can be used before the cloth must be washed is
    A. 500-1000   B. 2000-3000   C. 4000-6000   D. 8000-10000

29. A cleaning woman working a six-hour shift should be able to cover (clean) _____ Gilbert work units.
    A. 100-200   B. 400-500   C. 1100-1200   D. 6000-7000

30. An incipient fire is one which
    A. has just started and can be readily extinguished using an ordinary hand extinguisher
    B. occurs only in motor vehicles
    C. is burning out of control in a storeroom
    D. is a banked coal fire

31. Maintaining room temperature at 75°F in the winter time will increase fuel consumption above the amount needed to maintain 70°F by APPROXIMATELY
    A. 5%   B. 10%   C. 15%   D. 20%

32. Of the following, the one which represents the BEST practical combustion condition in an oil-fired low pressure steam plant is _____ stack temperature.
    A. 8% CO_2 - 500°F   B. 13% CO_2 - 400°F
    C. 10% CO_2 - 700°F   D. 6% CO_2 - 400°F

33. An office has floor dimensions of 6 ft. 6 in. wide by 22 ft. 0 in. long. The floor area of this office, in square feet, is MOST NEARLY
    A. 143   B. 263   C. 363   D. 463

34. Dollies are USUALLY used
    A. as convenient platforms upon which to store items
    B. as ornamental protective covers

C. to raise items to the required level
D. to transport items from one place to another

35. When lifting a heavy object from a table, which of the following rules is it MOST important to observe?
    A. Do not bend your knees.
    B. Do not stand too close to the object.
    C. Keep your back straight.
    D. Keep your shoulder level with the object

36. The FIRST objective of all fire prevention is
    A. confining fire to a limited area
    B. safeguarding life against fire
    C. reducing insurance rates
    D. preventing property damage

37. A custodian should know the equipment used in his work well enough to
    A. make any repairs which might be needed
    B. know what parts to remove in case of breakdown
    C. anticipate any reasonable possibility of a breakdown
    D. know all the lubricants specified by the manufacturer

38. The PRIMARY responsibility of a supervising custodian is to
    A. make friends of all subordinates
    B. search for new methods of doing the work
    C. win the respect of his superior
    D. get the work done properly within a reasonable time

39. When a custodian believes that the work of a subordinate is below standard, he should
    A. assign the employee to work that is considered undesirable
    B. do nothing immediately in the hope that the employee will bring his work up to standard without any help from the supervisor
    C. reduce the privileges of the employee at once
    D. discuss it as soon as possible with the employee

40. An office worker frequently complains to the custodian that her office is poorly illuminated.
    The BEST action for the custodian to follow is to
    A. ignore the complaints as those of an habitual crank
    B. inform the worker that illumination is a fixed item built into the building originally and evidently is the result of faulty planning by the architect
    C. request a licensed electrician to install additional ceiling lights
    D. investigate for faulty illumination features in the room, such as dirty lamp globes and incorrect lamp wattages

KEY (CORRECT ANSWERS)

1.	A	11.	D	21.	A	31.	D
2.	C	12.	D	22.	C	32.	B
3.	D	13.	A	23.	C	33.	C
4.	D	14.	D	24.	B	34.	D
5.	B	15.	B	25.	D	35.	C
6.	B	16.	A	26.	D	36.	B
7.	C	17.	B	27.	A	37.	C
8.	C	18.	A	28.	C	38.	D
9.	A	19.	B	29.	C	39.	D
10.	C	20.	B	30.	A	40.	D

TEST 2

DIRECTIONS: Each question or incomplete statement is followed by several suggested answers or completions. Select the one that BEST answers the question or completes the statement. *PRINT THE LETTER OF THE CORRECT ANSWER IN THE SPACE AT THE RIGHT.*

1. Of the following, the MOST important reason for the custodian to plan work schedules for men under his supervision is that
    A. emergency situations can easily be handled if they should arise
    B. it insures that essential operations will be adequately covered
    C. the men will be more satisfied if a routine is established
    D. the relationship between the supervisor and his subordinate will be clarified

    1._____

2. Sealers for open-grained wood floors should NOT contain linseed oil because
    A. the linseed oil would damage the wood fibers
    B. the linseed oil would deteriorate mop strands
    C. water wax would penetrate the linseed oil sealer and rot the wood
    D. linseed oil on wood take too long to dry satisfactorily before a floor finish could be applied

    2._____

3. When washing painted wall areas by hand, a man should be expected to wash each hour an area, in square feet, equal to
    A. 75-125   B. 150-300   C. 400-600   D. 750-1000

    3._____

4. Of the following, the one that is MOST desirable to use in dusting furniture is a
    A. feather duster   B. paper towel
    C. counter brush   D. soft cotton cloth

    4._____

5. The one of the following floor types on which oily sweeping compound may be used is
    A. vinyl tile   B. concrete   C. linoleum   D. terrazzo

    5._____

6. A steam heating system where the steam and condensate flow in the same pipe is called a _____ system.
    A. one pipe gravity return   B. sub-atmospheric
    C. vacuum return   D. zone control

    6._____

7. A test of a boiler by applying pressure equal to or greater than the maximum working pressure is called a _____ test.
    A. hydrostatic   B. barometric   C. hygroscopic   D. gyroscopic

    7._____

8. A stack switch, as used with an oil burner,
    A. shuts down the burner in case of non-ignition
    B. shuts down the burner in case of high stack temperatures
    C. controls the flow of secondary air
    D. operates the barometric damper

    8._____

9. The vertical pipes leading from the steam mains to the radiators are called 9._____
   A. drip lines
   B. risers
   C. radiant coils
   D. expansion joints

10. Fuel oil storage tanks are equipped with vents. 10._____
    The purpose of these vents is to
    A. make tank soundings
    B. check oil flash points
    C. fill the fuel tanks
    D. allow air to mix

11. A compound gauge in a boiler room 11._____
    A. measures steam and water pressure
    B. shows the quantity of boiler treatment compound on hand
    C. measures pressures above and below atmospheric pressure
    D. indicates the degree of compounding in a steam engine

12. Of the following, the CHIEF purpose of insulating steam lines is to 12._____
    A. prevent loss of heat
    B. protect people from being burned by them
    C. prevent leaks
    D. protect the pipes against corrosion

13. The MOST important function of thermostatic traps on radiators is to 13._____
    A. regulate the heat given off by the radiators
    B. remove water and air from the radiator
    C. assist the steam pressure in filling the radiator
    D. maintain a vacuum within the radiator

14. The designation *1/8-27N.P.T.* USUALLY indicates 14._____
    A. machine screw thread
    B. pipe thread
    C. spur gear size
    D. sprocket chain size

15. The size of a chisel is determined by its 15._____
    A. length   B. width   C. pitch   D. height

16. The cause of paint blisters is USUALLY 16._____
    A. moisture under the paint coat
    B. too thick a coat of paint
    C. too much oil in paint
    D. the plaster pores not sealed properly

17. A wood-framed picture is to be attached to a plaster and hollow tile wall. 17._____
    Of the following, the PROPER installation would include the use of
    A. wire cut nails
    B. miracle glue
    C. expansion shields and screws
    D. self-tapping screws

18. The PROPER tool or method to use for driving a finish nail to the depth necessary for puttying when installing wood trim is
    A. countersink
    B. another nail of the same diameter
    C. a nail set
    D. a center punch

19. Faucet leakage in a large building is BEST controlled by periodic
    A. faucet replacement
    B. addition of a sealing compound to the water supply
    C. packing replacement
    D. faucet inspection and repair

20. Escutcheons are USUALLY located
    A. on kitchen cabinet drawers
    B. on windows
    C. around pipes, to cover pipe sleeve openings
    D. around armored electric cable going into a gem box

21. It is ADVISABLE to remove broken bulbs from light sockets with
    A. a wooden or hard rubber wedge
    B. pliers
    C. a hammer and chisel
    D. a fuse puller

22. A room 20' x 25' in area with a ceiling height of 9'6" is to be painted. One gallon of paint will cover 400 square feet.
    The MINIMUM number of gallons necessary to give the four walls and the ceiling one coat of paint is
    A. 2 B. 3 C. 4 D. 5

23. Of the following, the ones on which gaskets are MOST likely to be used are
    A. threaded pipe plugs
    B. cast iron pipe nipples
    C. flanged pipe fittings
    D. threaded cast iron reducing tees

24. If a 110 volt lamp were used on a 220 volt circuit, the
    A. fuse would burn out
    B. lamp would burn out
    C. line would overheat
    D. lamp would flicker

25. The third prong on the plug of portable electric power tools of recent manufacture is for
    A. using the tool on a 3-phase power outlet
    B. eliminating interference in radio or television sets
    C. grounding the tool as a safety precaution
    D. using the tool on direct current circuits

26. When changing brushes on a scrubbing machine, of the following, the FIRST step to take is to
    A. lock the switch in the *off* position
    B. be sure the power cable electric plug supplying the machine is disconnected from the wall outlet
    C. place the machine on top of the positioned brushes
    D. dip the brushes in water

27. In cleaning away branches that have been broken off as a result of a severe storm, one of your men comes in contact with a live electric line and falls unconscious.
    After having removed him from contact, the FIRST thing to be done is to
    A. send for an inhalator to revive him
    B. administer mouth-to-mouth resuscitation
    C. search for the switch to prevent any other such cases
    D. loosen his clothing and begin rubbing his forehead to restore circulation

28. Of the following, the MOST effective way to reduce waste in cleaning equipment and tools is by
    A. requiring a worn brush or broom to be returned before issuing a new one
    B. requiring the cleaners to use all cleaning tools for specific periods of time
    C. keeping careful records of how frequently cleaning equipment and tools are issued to cleaners
    D. making sure that cleaners use the tools properly

29. A window cleaner should carefully examine his safety belt
    A. once a week
    B. before he puts it on each time
    C. once a month
    D. once before he enters a building

30. One of your cleaners was injured as a result of slipping on an oily floor.
    This type of accident is MOST likely due to
    A. defective equipment
    B. the physical condition of the cleaner
    C. failure to use proper safety appliances
    D. poor housekeeping

31. One important use of accident reports is to provide information that may be used to reduce the possibility of similar accidents.
    The MOST valuable entry on the report for this purpose is the
    A. name of the victim
    B. injury sustained by the victim
    C. cause of the accident
    D. location of the accident

32. Fires in buildings are of such complexity that
    A. no plans or methods of attack can be formulated in advance
    B. no planned procedures can be relied on
    C. an appointed committee is necessary to direct fighting at the fire
    D. the problem must be considered in advance and methods of attack formulated

33. Of the following types of fires, a soda-acid fire extinguisher is NOT recommended for
    A. electric motor controls
    B. waste paper
    C. waste rags
    D. wood desks

34. A foam-type fire extinguisher extinguishes fires by
    A. cooling only
    B. drenching only
    C. smothering only
    D. cooling and smothering

35. If a keg of nails had on it the words *Net Weight 10 pounds*, it would mean that the
    A. keg weighed 10 pounds without the nails
    B. nails and the keg together weighed 10 pounds
    C. nails weighed 10 pounds without the keg
    D. weight of 10 pounds is approximate

36. In deciding which items should be stored together, the one of the following factors which is usually of LEAST importance is
    A. activity
    B. class
    C. cost
    D. size

37. Of the following, the MOST effective way to teach a subordinate how to store an item is to
    A. do it yourself while explaining
    B. explain the procedure verbally
    C. have him do it while you criticize
    D. let him look at photographs of the operation

38. If a cleaner is doing excellent work, then the PROPER action of the custodian is to
    A. give him preferential assignments as a reward
    B. tell the other cleaners what excellent work he is doing
    C. praise his work at the earlies opportunity
    D. do nothing since the man may become over-confident

39. A cleaner does very good work, but he has trouble getting to work on time. To get the man to come on time, you should
    A. bring him up on charges to stop the lateness once and for all
    B. have him report directly to you every time he is late
    C. talk over the problem with him to find its cause and possible solution
    D. threaten to transfer him if he cannot get to work on time

40. When the National flag is to be flown at half staff, it should ALWAYS be hoisted
    A. slowly to half staff
    B. slowly to the peak of staff and then lowered slowly to half staff
    C. briskly to the peak of staff and then lowered slowly to half staff
    D. briskly to the peak of staff and then lowered briskly to half staff

KEY (CORRECT ANSWERS)

1.	B	11.	C	21.	A	31.	C
2.	D	12.	A	22.	C	32.	D
3.	B	13.	B	23.	C	33.	A
4.	D	14.	B	24.	B	34.	D
5.	B	15.	B	25.	C	35.	C
6.	A	16.		26.	B	36.	C
7.	A	17.	C	27.	B	37.	A
8.	A	18.	C	28.	D	38.	C
9.	B	19.	C	29.	B	39.	C
10.	D	20.	D	30.	D	40.	C

EXAMINATION SECTION
TEST 1

DIRECTIONS: Each question or incomplete statement is followed by several suggested answers or completions. Select the one that BEST answers the question or completes the statement. *PRINT THE LETTER OF THE CORRECT ANSWER IN THE SPACE AT THE RIGHT.*

1. Linseed oil is MOST commonly used to

   A. seal wooden floors
   B. polish brass fixtures
   C. thin exterior oil base paints
   D. lubricate fan bearings

1._____

2. The APPROXIMATE number of square feet of unobstructed corridor floorspace that one cleaner can sweep in an hour is

   A. 1200   B. 2400   C. 4000   D. 6000

2._____

3. Of the following materials, the one MOST effective in dusting office furniture is a

   A. silk cloth   B. chamois
   C. soft cotton cloth   D. counter brush

3._____

4. Of the following materials, the one that should be used to produce the MOST resilient flooring is

   A. concrete   B. terrazzo
   C. ceramic tile   D. asphalt tile

4._____

5. Sweeping compound is used on concrete floors MAINLY to

   A. keep the dust down
   B. polish the floor
   C. harden the floor surface
   D. indicate which part of the floor has not been swept

5._____

6. The type of floor finish or wax that will produce an anti-slip surface on resilient floor coverings is

   A. resin-based floor finish
   B. water emulsion wax
   C. paste wax
   D. paraffin

6._____

7. High sheen and good wearing qualities can be obtained when polishing a waxed floor by using an electric scrubbing machine equipped with

   A. nylon disks   B. soft brushes
   C. steel wool pads   D. pumice wheels

7._____

8. Spalling of the surface of a marble floor may result if the floor is washed with

   A. a solution of trisodium phosphate   B. a soft soap solution
   C. a neutral liquid detergent solution D. cold water

8._____

39

9. When not in use, a broom should be stored

   A. resting on the floor with the handle end down
   B. resting on the floor with the bristle end down
   C. hanging by the handle from a hook
   D. lying flat on the floor

10. The one of the following items which ordinarily requires the MOST time to wash is a(n)

    A. 5 ft x 10 ft Venetian blind
    B. 4 ft fluorescent fixture
    C. incandescent fixture
    D. 5 ft x 10 ft ceramic tile floor

11. A broom that has been properly used should GENERALLY be replaced after

    A. it has been used for one month
    B. its bristles have been worn down by more than one-third of their original length
    C. it has been used for two months
    D. its bristles have been worn down by more than two-thirds of their original length

12. The floor area of a room which measures 10 ft long x 10 ft wide is _____ sq. ft.

    A. 20   B. 40   C. 100   D. 1000

13. The FIRST thing that should be checked before an oil-fired, low-pressure steam boiler is started up in the morning is the

    A. boiler water level   B. stack temperature
    C. aquastat   D. vaporstat

14. The MAIN reason for preheating number 6 fuel oil before allowing it to enter an oil burner is to

    A. increase its viscosity
    B. decrease its viscosity
    C. increase its heating value
    D. decrease its flash point

15. A house pump is used to

    A. drain basements that become flooded
    B. pump sewage from the basement to the sewer
    C. pump city water to a roof storage tank
    D. circulate domestic hot water

16. The device which shuts down an automatic rotary cup oil burner when the steam pressure reaches a preset high limit is a

    A. pressure gage   B. pressurtrol
    C. safety valve   D. low water cutoff

17. A pressure gage connected to a compressed air tank USUALLY reads in   17.____

    A. pounds   B. pounds per square inch
    C. inches of mercury   D. feet of water

18. The device which shuts off the oil burner when the water level in the boiler is too low is   18.____
    the

    A. feedwater regulator   B. low water cutoff
    C. high water alarm   D. programmer

19. The device which shuts down an oil burner when there is a flame failure is the   19.____

    A. stack switch   B. thermostat
    C. manometer   D. modutrol motor

20. The switch which is used to shut off the oil burner in case of a fire in the boiler room is   20.____
    located

    A. on the programmer cover
    B. near the boiler room entrance
    C. on the burner motor
    D. in the custodian's office

21. The MOST likely reason for a cold water faucet to continue to drip after its washer has   21.____
    been replaced is a defective

    A. handle   B. stem   C. seat   D. bib

22. In water lines, the type of valve which should always be either fully open or fully closed is   22.____
    the

    A. needle valve   B. gate valve
    C. globe valve   D. mixing valve

23. The BEST tool to use on a 1" galvanized iron pipe nipple when unscrewing the nipple   23.____
    from a coupling is a _____ wrench.

    A. crescent   B. stillson   C. monkey   D. spud

24. The BEST way to locate a leak in a natural gas pipe line is to   24.____

    A. hold a lighted match under the pipe and move it along the length of the pipe slowly
    B. hold a lighted match about two inches above the pipe and move it along the length
       of the pipe slowly
    C. coat the pipe with a soapy solution and watch for bubbles
    D. shut off the gas at the meter and then coat the pipe with a soapy solution and
       watch for bubbles

25. When comparing a 60 watt yellow bulb with a 60 watt clear bulb, it can be said that they   25.____
    BOTH

    A. give the same amount of light
    B. use the same amount of power
    C. will burn for at least 60 hours
    D. will burn for at least 60 days

26. The output capacity of an electric motor is USUALLY rated in

   A. kilowatts
   B. horsepower
   C. percent
   D. cubic feet

27. A fuse will burn out whenever it is subjected to excessive

   A. resistance
   B. voltage
   C. current
   D. capacitance

28. Of the following, the device which uses the GREATEST amount of electric power is the

   A. electric typewriter
   B. $\frac{1}{4}$ inch electric drill
   C. floor scrubbing machine
   D. oil burner ignition transformer

29. Meters which indicate the electric power consumed in a public building are read in

   A. kilowatt-hours
   B. volts
   C. cubic feet
   D. degree days

30. Tongue and groove lumber is used for

   A. desk drawers
   B. hardwood floors
   C. picture frames
   D. cabinet doors

31. When hand sawing a 1" x 4" board parallel to the grain of the wood, the BEST saw to use is the _____ saw.

   A. cross-cut
   B. back
   C. hack
   D. rip

32. The BEST tool to use to make a recess for the head of a flat-head wood screw is a(n)

   A. counterbore
   B. countersink
   C. auger
   D. nail set

33. In attaching two pieces of wood with a nut and bolt, the holes drilled should be

   A. slightly undersize in one piece, slightly oversize in the other
   B. slightly oversize in both pieces
   C. slightly undersize in both pieces
   D. drilled from opposite sides of the joint

34. The one of the following transmission devices which should be oiled MOST often is the

   A. V-belt
   B. roller chain
   C. rigid coupling
   D. clutch plate

35. A motor-generator set is USUALLY part of a(n)

   A. steam boiler
   B. hydraulic elevator
   C. electric elevator
   D. incinerator

36. The one of the following devices which MOST frequently contains hydraulic fluid is a

   A. door closer
   B. worm gear reducer
   C. foam fire extinguisher
   D. hand winch

37. A breakdown of the causes of accidental injuries by percent would show that such injuries are *most nearly* caused

   A. 100 percent by unsafe physical working conditions
   B. 100 percent by unsafe acts of people
   C. 50 percent by unsafe physical working conditions and 50 percent by unsafe acts of people
   D. 20 percent by unsafe physical working conditions and 80 percent by unsafe acts of people

38. When using an eight-foot stepladder, a worker should climb up not more than _____ rungs.

   A. 4
   B. 5
   C. 6
   D. 7

39. A supervisor interested in the safety of his subordinates would NOT permit

   A. using a wooden rule to take measurements near electrical apparatus
   B. using a machinist's hammer to strike a chisel
   C. removing metal chips from a machine with a rag
   D. testing the heat of a soldering iron with a piece of solder

40. If a worker feels an electric shock while using a portable electric drill, he should immediately

   A. stand on a piece of scrap lumber
   B. reverse the plug in the receptacle
   C. hold onto a grounded pipe or piece of metal
   D. take the drill out of service

KEY (CORRECT ANSWERS)

1. C	11. B	21. C	31. D
2. D	12. C	22. B	32. B
3. C	13. A	23. B	33. B
4. D	14. A	24. C	34. B
5. A	15. C	25. B	35. C
6. A	16. B	26. B	36. A
7. B	17. B	27. C	37. D
8. A	18. B	28. C	38. C
9. C	19. A	29. A	39. C
10. A	20. B	30. B	40. D

TEST 2

DIRECTIONS: Each question or incomplete statement is followed by several suggested answers or completions. Select the one that BEST answers the question or completes the statement. *PRINT THE LETTER OF THE CORRECT ANSWER IN THE SPACE AT THE RIGHT.*

1. During a shortage of custodial help in a public building, the cleaning task which will probably receive LEAST attention is 1.____

    A. picking up sweepings
    B. emptying ashtrays
    C. washing walls
    D. dust-mopping offices

2. Of the following substances commonly used on floors, the MOST flammable is 2.____

    A. resin-based floor finish
    B. floor sealer
    C. water emulsion wax
    D. trisodium phosphate

3. The MOST effective method for cleaning badly soiled carpeting is 3.____

    A. wet shampooing
    B. vacuum cleaning
    C. dry shampooing
    D. wire brushing

4. Before repainting becomes necessary, a painted wall can USUALLY be washed completely 4.____

    A. only once
    B. two or three times
    C. eight to ten times
    D. sixteen to twenty times

5. The FIRST step in routine cleaning of offices at night should be 5.____

    A. sweeping floors
    B. emptying ashtrays
    C. dusting furniture
    D. damp mopping the floors

6. Among the factors pertaining to the maintenance and cleaning of a building, the one MOST likely to be under the control of the building custodian is the 6.____

    A. size of the area
    B. density of occupancy
    C. type of occupancy
    D. standards to be maintained

7. "Treated" or "dustless" sweeping of resilient-type floors requires 7.____

    A. spraying the floors with water to keep the dust down
    B. spreading sweeping compound on the floor
    C. sweeping cloths that are chemically treated with mineral oil
    D. spraying the sweeping tool with neatsfoot oil

8. A modern central vacuum cleaner system 8.____

    A. is cheaper to operate than one portable machine
    B. generally produces less suction than a portable machine
    C. conveys the dirt directly to a basement tank
    D. must be operated only in the daytime

9. Oxalic acid can be used to 9.____

   A. remove ink spots from wood
   B. clear floor drains
   C. solder copper flashing
   D. polish brass

10. The BEST material for sealing a terrazzo floor is 10.____

    A. varnish   B. a penetrating seal
    C. shellac   D. a surface seal

11. The MOST troublesome feature in cleaning public washrooms is 11.____

    A. cleaning and deodorizing the urinals
    B. washing the toilet bowls
    C. mopping the tile floors
    D. removing chewing gum from the floors

12. In order to improve its appearance, extend its life, and reduce the labor involved in dusting, wood furniture should be polished with 12.____

    A. an oil polish
    B. a water emulsion wax
    C. a silicone and spirit chemical spray
    D. clear water

13. Ringelmann charts are useful in determining 13.____

    A. interest rates
    B. smoke density
    C. standard times for cleaning operations
    D. fuel consumption

14. A fusible plug is USUALLY found in a 14.____

    A. lighting panel   B. fire door
    C. boiler wall   D. house tank

15. In an air conditioned office, MOST people would feel comfortable when the room temperature and humidity are maintained, respectively, at 15.____

    A. 75° F and 50%   B. 70° F and 30%
    C. 75° F and 20%   D. 65° F and 75%

16. The one of the following sets of conditions which will provide the MOST efficient combustion in an oil-fired low-temperature steam boiler is _____ stack temperature, _____ CO_2. 16.____

    A. 400° F, 12%   B. 500° F, 10%
    C. 600° F, 8%   D. 700° F, 6%

17. The BEST way for a building custodian to tell if the night cleaners have done their work well is to check

   A. on how much cleaning material has been used
   B. on how much waste paper was collected
   C. the building for cleanliness
   D. the floor mops to see if they are still wet

18. The one of the following which is the BEST reason for introducing a training program is that the

   A. quality of work is above standard
   B. employees are all experienced
   C. accident rate is too high
   D. tenant complaints are negligible

19. The FIRST step in training an inexperienced individual in a particular job is to

   A. put him to work and watch for mistakes
   B. put him to work and tell him to call for help if he needs it
   C. put him at ease and then find out what he knows about the work
   D. tell him to watch the least experienced worker on the job because the training is still fresh in his mind

20. As used in job analysis, the term "job breakdown" means

   A. any equipment failure
   B. any failure on the part of the worker to complete the job
   C. dividing the job into a series of steps
   D. reducing the number of workers by 50 percent

21. At times when a public building is closed to the public, the building custodian should

   A. keep all doors locked and admit no one
   B. admit only custodial employees
   C. admit anyone as long as he signs the log
   D. admit only those who have business in the building

22. When a public building is equipped for security purposes with exterior lights on or around the building, the lights should be kept lit

   A. all night except for Saturdays, Sundays, and holidays
   B. twenty-four hours a day on weekends
   C. throughout the night, every night of the week
   D. until midnight, every night of the week

23. Custodial workers are MOST liable to injury when they are engaged in

   A. sweeping floors   B. mopping floors
   C. dusting furniture   D. moving furniture

24. The BEST place to store a wooden stepladder is 24._____

    A. in a boiler room
    B. in a stairwell
    C. in a dry room
    D. outside a basement window provided that there is a locked grating overhead

25. Of the following, the BEST action for a building custodian to take when he notices that an office worker in his building has a hot plate connected to a heavily loaded electric circuit is to 25._____

    A. remove the hot plate from the office when its owner is not present
    B. demand that the office worker remove the hot plate immediately
    C. write a report to the supervisor of the office requesting corrective action
    D. ignore the situation

26. In dealing with the public, a building custodian should be 26._____

    A. indulgent
    B. courteous
    C. disagreeable
    D. unavailable

27. If a building custodian sees a group of people in front of his building preparing to form a picket line, he should 27._____

    A. turn on a lawn sprinkler to spray the pickets
    B. order the pickets off the sidewalk in front of the building
    C. show the pickets he is sympathetic with their complaint
    D. contact his supervisor immediately for instructions

28. When electric service in a public building is to be shut off from 10 A.M. Tuesday to 11:30 the next morning because a new electric feeder cable is being installed, the building custodian should 28._____

    A. prepare a memo to all office supervisors in the building, notifying them of the situation, and deliver a copy to each office as soon as possible
    B. prepare a notice of the impending power stoppage and post it in the lobby early Tuesday morning
    C. tell the electrical contractor to notify the tenants when he is about to shut off the power
    D. discontinue elevator service at 10 A.M. on Tuesday as an indication to the tenants that the power supply is off

29. The BEST way to remove some small pieces of broken glass from a floor is to 29._____

    A. use a brush and dustpan
    B. pick up the pieces carefully with your hands
    C. use a wet mop and a wringer
    D. sweep the pieces into the corner of the room

30. There is a two-light fixture in the room where you are working. One of the light bulbs goes out, and you need more light to work by. You should 30._____

    A. change the fuse in the fuse box
    B. have a new bulb put in
    C. call for an electrician and stop work till he comes
    D. find out what is causing the short circuit

31. While working on the job, you accidently break a window pane. No one is around, and you are able to clean up the broken pieces of glass. It would then be BEST for you to

    A. leave a note near the window that a new glass has to be put in because it was accidently broken
    B. forget about the whole thing because the window was not broken on purpose
    C. write a report to your supervisor telling him that you saw a broken window pane that has to be fixed
    D. tell your supervisor that you accidently broke the window pane while working

32. Many machines have certain safety devices for the operators. The MOST important reason for having these safety devices is to

    A. increase the amount of work that the machines can do
    B. permit repairs to be made on the machines without shutting them down
    C. help prevent accidents to people who use the machines
    D. reduce the cost of electric power needed to run the machines

Questions 33-36.

DIRECTIONS: Answer Questions 33 through 36 only according to the information given in the following passage.

MOPPING FLOORS

When mopping hardened cement floors, either painted or unpainted, a soap and water mixture should be used. This should be made by dissolving 1/2 a cup of soft soap in a pail of hot water. It is not desirable, however, under any circumstances, to use a soap and water mixture on cement floors that are not hardened. For mopping this type of floor, it is recommended that the cleaning agent be made up of 2 ounces of laundry soda mixed in a pail of water.

Soaps are not generally used on hard tile floors because slippery films may build up on the floor. It is generally recommended that these floors be mopped using a pail of hot water in which has been mixed 2 ounces of washing powder for each gallon of water. The floors should then be rinsed thoroughly.

After the mopping is finished, proper care should be taken of the mop. This is done by first cleaning the mop in clear warm water. Then it should be wrung out, after which the strands of the mop should be untangled. Finally, the mop should be hung by its handle to dry.

33. According to the above passage, you should NEVER use a soap and water mixture when mopping _____ floors.

    A. hardened cement   B. painted
    C. unhardened cement D. unpainted

34. According to the above passage, using laundry soda mixed in a pail of water as a cleaning agent is recommended for

    A. all floors
    B. all floors except hard tile floors
    C. some cement floors
    D. linoleum floor coverings only

35. According to the above passage, the GENERALLY recommended mixture for mopping hard tile floors is

   A. 1/2 cup of soft soap for each gallon of hot water
   B. 1/2 cup of soft soap in a pail of hot water
   C. 2 ounces of washing powder in a pail of hot water
   D. 2 ounches of washing powder for each gallon of hot water

36. According to the above passage, the PROPER care of a mop after it is used includes

   A. cleaning it in clear cold water and hanging it by its handle to dry
   B. wringing it out, untangling, and drying it
   C. untangling its strands before wringing it out
   D. untangling its strands while cleaning it in clear water

Questions 37-40.

DIRECTIONS: Answer Questions 37 through 40 only according to the information given in the following passage.

ACCIDENT PREVENTION

Many accidents and injuries can be prevented if employees learn to be move careful. The wearing of shoes with thin or badly worn soles or open toes can easily lead to foot injuries from tacks, nails, and chair and desk legs. Loose or torn clothing should not be worn near moving machinery. This is especially true of neckties which can very easily become caught in the machine. You should not place objects so that they block or partly block hallways, corridors, or other passageways. Even when they are stored in the proper place, tools, supplies, and equipment should be carefully placed or piled so as not to fall, nor have anything stick out from a pile. Before cabinets, lockers or ladders are moved, the tops should be cleared of anything which might injure someone or fall off. If necessary, use a dolly to move these or other bulky objects.

Despite all efforts to avoid accidents and injuries, however, some will happen. If an employee is injured, no matter how small the injury, he should report it to his supervisor and have the injury treated. A small cut that is not attended to can easily become infected and can cause more trouble than some injuries which at first seem more serious. It never pays to take chances.

37. According to the above passage, the one statement that is NOT true is that

   A. by being more careful, employees can reduce the number of accidents that happen
   B. women should wear shoes with open toes for comfort when working
   C. supplies should be piled so that nothing is sticking out from the pile
   D. if an employee sprains his wrist at work, he should tell his supervisor about it

38. According to the above passage, you should NOT wear loose clothing when you are

   A. in a corridor
   B. storing tools
   C. opening cabinets
   D. near moving machinery

39. According to the above passage, before moving a ladder, you should 39.____
   A. test all the rungs
   B. get a dolly to carry the ladder at all times
   C. remove everything from the top of the ladder which might fall off
   D. remove your necktie

40. According to the above passage, an employee who gets a slight cut should 40.____
   A. have it treated to help prevent infection
   B. know that a slight cut becomes more easily infected than a big cut
   C. pay no attention to it as it can't become serious
   D. realize that it is more serious than any other type of injury

KEY (CORRECT ANSWERS)

1. C	11. A	21. D	31. D
2. B	12. C	22. C	32. C
3. A	13. B	23. D	33. C
4. B	14. C	24. C	34. C
5. B	15. A	25. C	35. D
6. D	16. A	26. B	36. B
7. C	17. C	27. D	37. B
8. C	18. C	28. A	38. D
9. A	19. C	29. A	39. C
10. B	20. C	30. B	40. A

TEST 3

DIRECTIONS: Each question or incomplete statement is followed by several suggested answers or completions. Select the one that BEST answers the question or completes the statement. *PRINT THE LETTER OF THE CORRECT ANSWER IN THE SPACE AT THE RIGHT.*

1. An electric motor fire should be put out with an extinguisher that uses 1.____

    A. carbon dioxide
    B. soda-acid
    C. foam
    D. a pump tank

2. The charge in a soda-acid fire extinguisher should be replaced once 2.____

    A. a month
    B. every three months
    C. every six months
    D. a year

3. An elevator machinery room should have a fire extinguisher of the _____ type. 3.____

    A. soda-acid
    B. foam
    C. carbon dioxide
    D. sand pail

4. The national flag should be raised 4.____

    A. slowly and lowered briskly
    B. briskly and lowered slowly
    C. briskly and lowered briskly
    D. slowly and lowered slowly

5. The material which is used to seal the outside edges of a pane of window glass is 5.____

    A. stellite
    B. putty
    C. plastic wood
    D. caulking compound

6. The ceiling of a room which measures 20 ft x 30 ft is to be given two coats of paint. If one gallon of paint will cover 500 square feet, the two coats of paint will require a MINIMUM of _____ gallons. 6.____

    A. 1.5   B. 2   C. 2.4   D. 3.2

7. Rubbish, sticks, and papers on the lawn in front of a building should be collected by using a 7.____

    A. rake
    B. broom
    C. paper sticker
    D. hoe

8. Mortar stains on brickwork can be scrubbed off by using a solution of 8.____

    A. benzine
    B. tri-sodium phosphate
    C. muriatic acid
    D. acetic acid

9. The BEST chemical for melting ice on sidewalks is 9.____

    A. sodium chloride
    B. calcium carbonate
    C. hydrogen sulphide
    D. calcium chloride

51

10. Before painting a kitchen wall,

    A. a degreaser must be mixed with the paint
    B. all traces of grease must be washed off
    C. a water-base paint must be used to dissolve the grease
    D. the walls must be sanded to remove all traces of grease and old paint

11. For interior walls which must be washed very often, the PREFERRED paint is

    A. enamel B. flat
    C. exterior varnish D. calsomine

12. A type of window which is USUALLY equipped with sash cords or chains is the _____ type.

    A. hopper B. awning
    C. casement D. double-hung

13. The slats of a Venetian blind are usually tilted by a device containing a _____ gear.

    A. worm B. spur C. hypoid D. bevil

14. When washing the outside of a window with a narrow inside sill, a window cleaner should place his water pail on

    A. the outside window sill
    B. the nearest desk or chair
    C. a radiator at the center of the window
    D. the floor at a convenient point toward one side of the window

15. In order to determine the carrying capacity of a passenger elevator, a custodian would have to

    A. measure the floor area
    B. check the diameter of the cable
    C. read the inspection certificate
    D. read the motor nameplate

16. Before pruning a tree, the FIRST step should be to determine

    A. if there is insect infestation
    B. the general health of the tree
    C. the desired results
    D. amount of excess foliage

17. Tree fertilizer should have a high content of

    A. slaked lime B. chlordane
    C. rose dust D. nitrogen

18. A gasoline-driven snow blower should be stored for the summer with its fuel tank

    A. filled with gasoline
    B. and fuel lines drained
    C. filled with water
    D. half filled with number 4 fuel oil

19. A pipe that "sweats" in the summer time PROBABLY contains

    A. hot water
    B. low pressure steam
    C. domestic gas
    D. cold water

20. A good preventive maintenance program requires that each item of equipment be

    A. represented by an up-to-date record card on file
    B. lubricated daily
    C. brand new at the start of the program
    D. painted inside and out

Questions 21-24.

DIRECTIONS: Questions 21 through 24, inclusive, are to be answered SOLELY on the basis of the following paragraph.

All cleaning agents and supplies should be kept in a central storeroom which should be kept looked and only the custodian, storekeeper and foreman should have keys. Shelving should be provided for the smaller items, while barrels containing scouring powder or other bulk material should be set on the floor or on special cradles. Each compartment in the shelves should be marked plainly and only the item indicated stored therein. Each barrel should also be marked plainly. It may also be desirable to keep special items such as electric lamps, flashlight batteries, etc., in a locked cabinet or separate room to which only the custodian and the night building foreman have keys.

21. According to the above paragraph, scouring powder

    A. should be kept on shelves
    B. comes in one-pound cans
    C. should be kept in a locked cabinet
    D. is a bulk material

22. According to the above paragraph,

    A. the storekeeper should not be entrusted with the safekeeping of light bulbs
    B. flashlight batteries should be stored in barrels
    C. the central storeroom should be kept locked
    D. only special items should be stored under lock and key

23. According to the above paragraph,

    A. each shelf compartment should contain at least four different items
    B. barrels must be stored in cradles
    C. all items stored should be in marked compartments
    D. crates of light bulbs should be stored in cradles

24. As used in the above paragraph, the word *cradle* means a

    A. dolly
    B. support
    C. doll's bed
    D. hand truck

Questions 25-28.

DIRECTIONS: Questions 25 through 28, inclusive, are to be answered SOLELY on the basis of the following paragraph.

There are on the market many cleaning agents for which amazing claims are made. Chemical analysis shows that the majority of them are well-known chemicals slightly modified and packaged and sold under various trade names. For that reason, the agents which have been selected for your use are those whose cleaning properties are well-known and whose use can be standardized. It is obviously undesirable to offer too wide a selection as that would be confusing to the cleaner, but a sufficient number must be provided so that a satisfactory agent is available for each task.

25. According to the above paragraph,
   A. there are few cleaning agents on the market
   B. there are no really good cleaning agents on the market
   C. cleaning agents are sold under several different brand names
   D. all cleaning agents are the same

26. According to the above paragraph,
   A. all cleaning agents should be chemically analyzed before use
   B. the best cleaning agents are those for which no claims are made by the manufacturer
   C. different cleaning agents may be needed for different tasks
   D. all cleaning agents have been standardized by the federal government

27. As used in the above paragraph, the word *amazing* means
   A. illegal   B. untrue
   C. astonishing   D. specific

28. As used in the above paragraph, the word *modified* means
   A. changed   B. refined   C. labelled   D. diluted

29. The MAIN reason for keeping an inventory of housekeeping supplies is to
   A. be sure that supplies are available when needed
   B. determine the cost of the supplies
   C. automatically prevent waste of the supplies
   D. be sure that at least two years' supplies are on hand at all times

30. Current daily records are MOST desirable in dealing with problems concerning
   A. accidents
   B. vandalism
   C. employee time and attendance
   D. the consumption of electricity

31. The continuous record of activities taking place in a boiler room is called a
   A. computer   B. data bank
   C. log book   D. time sheet

32. The one of the following subjects of a fire prevention training program which is MOST readily applied on the job is the

    A. elimination of fire hazards
    B. use of portable fire extinguishers
    C. knowledge of types of fires
    D. method of reporting fires

33. A good supervisor will NOT

    A. tell his men what their jobs are and why they are important
    B. show his men how their jobs are to be done in the right way
    C. require some of the men to do their jobs in the presence of the supervisor demonstrating that they understand the job
    D. leave his men alone because they will always do their jobs correctly once they have received their instructions

34. When a supervisor sees a worker doing his job incorrectly, he should

    A. tell the worker to be more careful
    B. suspend the worker until he learns to do the job correctly
    C. tell the worker specifically how the job should be done
    D. scold the man

35. An office worker complains to a custodian that one of the cleaners broke off a branch of a plant which she kept on her desk and that she can identify the cleaner.
    The BEST thing for the custodian to do is to

    A. convince her that the plant will grow another branch eventually
    B. make the cleaner apologize and pay for a new plant out of his own pocket
    C. sympathize with the office worker and assure her that he will speak to the cleaner about it
    D. tell her not to bother him about her personal property

36. An employee who is a good worker but is often late for work

    A. is lazy and should be dismissed
    B. cannot tell time
    C. can have no excuse for being late more than once a month
    D. should be questioned by his supervisor to try to find out why he is late

37. When starting any disciplinary action, a good supervisor should

    A. show his annoyance by losing his temper
    B. be apologetic
    C. be sarcastic
    D. be firm and positive

38. Good public relations can be damaged by a custodian who treats tenants, fellow workers, friends, relatives, and the public with

    A. courtesy   B. consideration
    C. contempt   D. respect

39. The BEST way for a supervisor to maintain good employee morale is to

    A. avoid praising any one employee
    B. always have an alibi for his own mistakes
    C. encourage cliques by given them information before giving it to other workers
    D. give adequate credit and praise when due

40. When a new employee reports to a custodian on his first day on the job, the custodian should

    A. extend a hearty welcome and make the new employee feel welcome
    B. have the man sit and wait for a while before seeing him so that the employee realizes how busy the custodian is
    C. warn him of stern disciplinary action if he is late or absent excessively
    D. tell him he probably will have difficulty doing the work so that he doesn't become overconfident

---

KEY (CORRECT ANSWERS)

1. A	11. A	21. D	31. C
2. D	12. D	22. C	32. A
3. C	13. A	23. C	33. D
4. B	14. D	24. B	34. C
5. B	15. C	25. C	35. C
6. C	16. C	26. C	36. D
7. A	17. D	27. C	37. D
8. C	18. B	28. A	38. C
9. D	19. D	29. A	39. D
10. B	20. A	30. C	40. A

EXAMINATION SECTION
TEST 1

DIRECTIONS: Each question or incomplete statement is followed by several suggested answers or completions. Select the one that BEST answers the question or completes the statement. *PRINT THE LETTER OF THE CORRECT ANSWER IN THE SPACE AT THE RIGHT.*

1. The BEST course of action to take to settle a job-related dispute that has arisen among two of your employees is to

   A. bring them both together, listen to their arguments, and then make a decision
   B. tell the two employees individually to settle their dispute
   C. tell both employees to submit their dispute in writing to you and then make a decision
   D. listen to the argument of each one separately and then make a decision

   1.____

2. A custodian accidentally discovers a bottle of whiskey in a staff member's desk. The BEST procedure for the custodian to follow is to

   A. verbally reprimand him and prefer departmental charges
   B. inform him that whiskey is not allowed in school buildings
   C. call a meeting of all the employees and tell them what you found
   D. do nothing as you do not want to embarrass the person

   2.____

3. A new employee under your supervision constantly reports late for work. The one of the following actions you should take FIRST is to

   A. admonish him in front of the other employees
   B. prefer charges against him
   C. transfer him to another school
   D. warn him that he must be on time

   3.____

4. The one of the following procedures that is BEST to follow when it is necessary to reprimand a worker is to

   A. issue the same reprimand to all your men
   B. avoid him so he won't feel bad
   C. speak to him privately about the matter
   D. tell him what he has done wrong immediately to teach the other employees a lesson

   4.____

5. The LEAST important factor to consider when evaluating the work of an employee is

   A. his grade on his civil service test
   B. the quality of his work
   C. his resourcefulness
   D. his attendance record

   5.____

6. The one of the following supervisory actions that a custodian should use LEAST often is to

    A. make periodic reports to his superior about the work of his men
    B. bring employees up on "charges" whenever they do anything wrong
    C. listen to staff grievances
    D. advise an employee concerning a personal problem

7. The MAIN supervisory responsibility of a custodian is to

    A. foster policies of the board and the parents' organizations
    B. do his job so well that the students and employees like him
    C. make assignments to his employees
    D. keep the building and grounds in good operating condition

8. One of your employees verbally protests to you about your evaluation of his work. The BEST way to handle him is to

    A. advise him of your lengthy and qualified experience
    B. tell him that you do not care to talk about it
    C. explain to him how you arrived at your evaluation
    D. tell him that since all the other employees are satisfied, he should withdraw his complaint

9. A custodian will BEST keep the morale of his men high by

    A. giving praise for well-done work
    B. assigning good workers the most work
    C. personally helping each man in all the details of the man's job
    D. allowing special privileges for good work

10. In training maintenance personnel under the supervision of a custodian, the one of the following that should be given LEAST consideration by the custodian is

    A. how the training is to be given
    B. who is to be trained
    C. when the training will be given
    D. how the school principal wants them to be trained

11. The BEST attitude for a custodian to follow in his dealings with the public is to

    A. offer aid and cooperation to the public wherever possible
    B. show authority so that the public knows the limits to which they may make requests
    C. ignore the public since the custodian has a specific job to do
    D. refer the public to higher authority for solution of all their problems

12. The students playing in the schoolyard consistently lose rubber balls that land on the school roof. They request that you, the custodian, retrieve these balls
    Of the following, the BEST procedure for you to follow is .

    A. teach them a lesson and refuse to retrieve the balls
    B. retrieve the balls and throw them into the incinerator
    C. one day a week retrieve the balls and return them to the students
    D. retrieve the balls and give them to a local children's charity

13. The president of a charitable organization requests a permit to use the school building. You, the custodian, note that this same organization used the school previously and did not observe the "no smoking" rules.
    The BEST procedure for you to follow is to

    A. deny the organization a permit since they did not obey the school regulations before
    B. issue the permit without any questions since a large group is difficult to control
    C. inform the president that if any of his members continue to disregard the "no smoking" rules, future permits will not be issued
    D. inform the president that if any of his members continue to disregard the "no smoking" rules, you will evict them from the school building

14. Due to some grievances, parents occupy your school on a weekend and refuse to leave. As the school principal is out of town and unavailable, the BEST procedure for you, the custodian on duty, is to

    A. tell your employees to vacate the school
    B. call the police department
    C. cooperate with the parents on the take-over
    D. lock all the people in the school

15. An organization requests a permit to use the school auditorium from the hours of 7 P.M. to 10 P.M. on a Tuesday evening. The organization also requests that its members be allowed to enter the school earlier than 7 P.M. and leave later than 10 P.M.
    The BEST procedure for you, the custodian, to follow is to

    A. inform the organization leader that the organization may only use the school from the hours of 7 P.M. to 10 P.M.
    B. issue the permit without saying anything as you want to maintain good public relations
    C. refer the matter to the school principal as you do not want to get involved
    D. ask the organization leader the reasons for the request and, if the request is fair, issue the permit and let the organization do as it pleases

16. Dog owners in the neighborhood have been disregarding the *curb your dog* signs and walking their dogs on your school lawn. You find that this interferes with the operation of powered lawn mowing equipment.
    Your BEST procedure to follow is to

    A. put up a higher fence
    B. chase the people and dogs away
    C. tell the owners you will call the police department
    D. explain the problem to the owners and ask them to curb their dogs

17. A cleaner reports to the custodian that a particular schoolroom is consistently messy and dirty. The one who is equally at fault as the students for this dirty room is the

    A. students' parents
    B. regular classroom teacher
    C. student peer groups
    D. cleaner for reporting the matter

18. A parent walks into a custodian's office and starts to shout at him about a claimed injustice to her child. The PROPER procedure for the custodian to follow is to

    A. call the police department
    B. summon the security guards
    C. vacate the office
    D. escort the parent to a guidance counselor

19. A newspaper reporter visiting a school should normally be referred to the

    A. school principal
    B. school custodian engineer
    C. assistant superintendent of schools
    D. borough supervisor of school custodians

20. The parents of children in the neighborhood of your school complain to you that their children cannot use the school playground after school hours because the gates are closed. The BEST procedure for you to follow is

    A. tell the parents the gates will remain closed after school hours
    B. arrange for the children to use a play street
    C. tell the parents to meet with the board on this matter
    D. try to arrange for the school gates to be open to a later hour after school hours

21. Assume that there is a regulation requiring the men to notify the custodian when they intend to be absent. One of your men stays out without notifying you.
    Of the following, the FIRST thing that you should do is to

    A. discuss the matter with your supervisor
    B. find out the reason for the man's failure to comply with this regulation
    C. threaten the man with disciplinary action
    D. find out what the other custodians are doing about similar situations

22. The members of a crew are LEAST likely to object to strict rules as long as

    A. they know who made them
    B. the rules are applied only occasionally as a disciplinary measure
    C. the rules are applied equally to all the workers
    D. they are posted in a public place

23. Your supervisor complains to you that he could not find you at your assigned location and that the crew under your supervision was idle while you were away.
    Of the following, it is MOST important for you to

    A. improve your supervisory practices
    B. warn the men to look busy whenever they see one of the bosses
    C. disregard such an unreasonable complaint
    D. make certain you are rarely away from your assigned location

5 (#1)

24. Assume that the crew you supervise considers some of their routine work unpleasant. The BEST way to get these unpleasant tasks done is to

    A. rotate them among all your men
    B. assign them to easygoing workers who never complain
    C. use them as a means of disciplining habitual latecomers
    D. do them yourself

25. Assume that when a custodian arrives at a job location, he finds that a loud argument is going on between two of his men.
    Of the following, the MOST advisable action for him to take first is to

    A. send one of the men to another job
    B. find out what caused the argument
    C. ask one of the other men to tell him the cause of the argument
    D. take the men with him to his supervisor

24.____

25.____

KEY (CORRECT ANSWERS)

1.	A	11.	A
2.	B	12.	C
3.	D	13.	C
4.	C	14.	B
5.	A	15.	A
6.	B	16.	D
7.	D	17.	B
8.	C	18.	D
9.	A	19.	A
10.	D	20.	D

21.	B
22.	C
23.	A
24.	A
25.	B

TEST 2

DIRECTIONS: Each question or incomplete statement is followed by several suggested answers or completions. Select the one that BEST answers the question or completes the statement. *PRINT THE LETTER OF THE CORRECT ANSWER IN THE SPACE AT THE RIGHT.*

1. Of the following, the BEST reason for a custodian NOT allowing his employees to accept tips from people is that

    A. all employees would not be given equal treatment
    B. employees would become dishonest
    C. people are entitled to service without tips
    D. people in projects can't afford tips

    1.___

2. Your attitude as a custodian to complaints by your employees should be that

    A. all employees like to complain
    B. if you let the worker "give off some steam," the complaint will disappear
    C. you will listen to them and try to correct the condition
    D. you will try to show the worker where he is wrong

    2.___

3. A requisition would be filled out by a custodian in order to

    A. get supplies from the stockroom
    B. return to the stockroom supplies you haven't used
    C. find out the supplies you have on hand
    D. show that supplies were used up faster than expected

    3.___

4. Assume that you are a custodian and have to write a report on a new employee who will finish his probationary period next month.
    Which one of the following would be the BEST reason for recommending that he be dropped from the job? He

    A. was late several times during the past five months for a total of 50 minutes
    B. is a slow worker compared to the other men
    C. insists on eating his lunch alone instead of with the other men
    D. is in the habit of accepting drinks from outsiders during working hours although you have often told him it is forbidden

    4.___

5. It is MOST important that a report from a custodian to his superior be

    A. typewritten
    B. free of any mistakes in spelling or English
    C. accurate and have all the necessary facts
    D. brief to save time of all concerned

    5.___

6. Suppose that you are a custodian and one of your men asks why you did not recommend him for an above-average work performance rating.
    You should tell him

    A. that above-average work reports can be recommended only by higher authority
    B. why you did not give him an above-average work report
    C. that you will recommend an above-average work performance rating next year if he does better work
    D. how he can appeal his rating and help him write his appeal

    6.___

62

7. Suppose that you are a custodian and one of your men is absent from work one day. You don't have any extra men and some of the work usually done by the absent man has to be finished that day.
   It would be BEST for you to

   A. call your men together and let them decide which one is to do the work
   B. shorten the lunch period and have each man do some of the work
   C. ask one of your better men to *pitch in* by doing a little extra work today
   D. explain to the buildings superintendent why it will not be possible to finish this work today

8. One of your men complains about a job you gave him. He is angry about getting the assignment. You don't think that the man is right in getting so upset.
   You should

   A. discuss the problem with him and explain why you gave him the job
   B. refer the man to your supervisor because he refuses to obey orders
   C. show the man that the whole matter is unimportant and a waste of time
   D. tell the man to do the job first and complain later

9. Two of your men start an argument while at work. As a custodian, you should

   A. ignore them; it is normal for men working together to have arguments
   B. stop them right away and find out what started the argument
   C. let them argue it out as long as they continue working and don't talk too loud
   D. speak to one of the men privately and tell him he is interfering with the work

10. Suppose you are a new custodian and you are put in charge of a crew of men whom you do not know and who have been working together for a few months.
    For a smooth changeover to your leadership, it would be BEST for you to

    A. let them continue working at their present assignments while you get to know them better
    B. tell the men to call their old supervisor if they have any trouble while you are learning the job
    C. ask the most experienced man to take charge of the crew for a short while until you are more familiar with the work
    D. ask each man whether he is satisfied with what he is doing or wants a change

11. One of your men makes a suggestion for improving the method of doing the work. You don't think the suggestion is workable.
    You should, as a custodian,

    A. forget the idea since it isn't workable
    B. tell the man to try out the idea and hold him responsible if it doesn't work out
    C. discuss with the man why you think the idea won't work and praise him for his interest in the job
    D. point out to the man that he is wasting your time bringing up an idea that is not practical

12. Suppose that you and your supervisor are making an inspection of one of the buildings you are responsible for cleaning. Your superior notices that the elevator in the building has not been cleaned. You know that a new employee who has been on the job for only three months is assigned
to this building. You should

    A. tell your supervisor that you will have the elevator cleaned and see that it is kept clean in the future
    B. explain to your supervisor the trouble you have in training new employees
    C. find the new man and ask him to explain to you and your superior why the elevator is not clean
    D. tell your supervisor that the elevator was clean when you made your last inspection

13. Suppose that your men were asked to work overtime in order to repair a water main break. When the work is finished, your superior thanks you for the excellent work that was done.
For you, a custodian, to tell your men about this would be

    A. *bad,* because this was a private conversation between you and your superior
    B. *good,* because your men will see that you are well-liked by your superior
    C. *bad,* because your men will think that they will be asked to work whenever there is an emergency
    D. *good,* because it will show the men their cooperation is appreciated

14. When you, as a custodian, discuss a grievance with an employee, you should

    A. not tell the employee what you think of his complaint until a later date
    B. avoid any arguments with the employee
    C. convince the employee that there is no basis for this grievance
    D. tell the employee his complaint is justified

15. At a quarter to five, one of your employees tells you that the incinerator in his building has much refuse in it and he is willing to work overtime to burn it.
If you give him permission to do this, it would be

    A. *good,* because it will save time the next day for other important work
    B. *bad,* because this is not an emergency for which overtime could be approved
    C. *good,* because tenants would not complain that refuse piles up and causes odors
    D. *bad,* because the law does not allow burning after 5:00 P.M.

16. Because of absences, you are left short-handed.
Which one of the following operations should you lay over so that you can cover the MOST important work on a minimum basis?

    A. Incineration of garbage
    B. Sweeping the lobby
    C. Sweeping and washing the elevators
    D. Washing corridor windows

17. Suppose that one of your men who is doing good work asks for a transfer to another custodian.
It would be BEST for you to

    A. have a private talk with the man to find out why he wants a transfer
    B. tell the man that the other custodian will also expect him to do good work
    C. approve the transfer without question because a dissatisfied man will do a poor job
    D. ask the other men in your crew if they are dissatisfied with your supervision

18. One of your experienced workers and a new employee are arguing about the correct way to do a job on which they are working together.
As a custodian, you should

    A. listen to both men and then tell them that they must learn to settle their argument without interrupting your work
    B. side with the older worker because he is more experienced
    C. listen to both men and then tell them how the work is to be done
    D. take one of the men off the job

19. Suppose that the department is introducing a new procedure for cleaning the hallways of buildings.
As a custodian, the BEST way for you to acquaint your men with this new procedure and to get them to use it is to

    A. wait until it has been tried out in another building and, if it is successful, put it into use in your building
    B. give each man a printed copy of the new procedure and set a deadline date by which each man is to read it and know it
    C. get your men together and explain the new procedure to them and how it will affect their work
    D. teach it to your best man and when he is familiar with it, ask him to teach it to the other men one at a time

20. Suppose that, as a custodian, you have finished *breaking in* a new employee. A few days later, you see the new man doing the job the wrong way.
You should

    A. immediately show the man what he is doing wrong and how to do it correctly
    B. assign him to some other work
    C. let your superior know that the new man cannot follow instructions
    D. say nothing because you may make the new man nervous

21. Suppose that a new type waxing machine is to be used in your building.
Of the following, the BEST way for you to teach your men how to use this machine is to

    A. give a talk on how to operate the machine
    B. demonstrate the operation and then have each man operate the machine under your supervision
    C. have the manufacturer give a talk on how to operate the machine
    D. give each man a set of carefully written instructions on how to operate the machine

22. When a custodian has to teach a man a new job, it would be MOST helpful for him to find out

    A. how long the man has been with the department and how long he plans to stay
    B. the man's dependability and willingness
    C. the man's past record of cooperation with other workers
    D. what the man already knows that will help him in learning the new job

23. When a new custodian comes on the job, it is LEAST important for him to know

    A. the location of the buildings in the unit
    B. how long the foremen have been there
    C. the names of the men who work there
    D. where the tools and equipment are kept

24. When you assign work to your men, it is usually BEST to

    A. give each man the same amount of work
    B. give the jobs that take the longest time to the senior men
    C. assign work to each man according to his ability
    D. let each man pick his own assignment

25. As a custodian, you will MOST likely be respected by your men if you

    A. keep your personnel records simple and clear
    B. offer them advice in solving their family problems
    C. leave it to them to decide how a job is to be done
    D. are fair and honest with them

KEY (CORRECT ANSWERS)

1.	C	11.	C
2.	C	12.	A
3.	A	13.	D
4.	D	14.	B
5.	C	15.	D
6.	B	16.	D
7.	C	17.	A
8.	A	18.	C
9.	B	19.	C
10.	A	20.	A

21. B
22. D
23. B
24. C
25. D

TEST 3

DIRECTIONS: Each question or incomplete statement is followed by several suggested answers or completions. Select the one that BEST answers the question or completes the statement. *PRINT THE LETTER OF THE CORRECT ANSWER IN THE SPACE AT THE RIGHT.*

1. Good public relations can be damaged by a custodian who treats tenants, fellow workers, friends, relatives, and the public with   1.___

   A. courtesy
   B. consideration
   C. contempt
   D. respect

2. An office worker complains to a custodian that one of the cleaners broke off a branch of a plant which she kept on her desk and that she can identify the cleaner.   2.___
   The BEST thing for the custodian to do is to

   A. convince her that the plant will grow another branch eventually
   B. make the cleaner apologize and pay for a new plant out of his own pocket
   C. sympathize with the office worker and assure her that he will speak to the cleaner about it
   D. tell her not to bother him about her personal property

3. When a new employee reports to a custodian on his first day on the job, the custodian SHOULD   3.___

   A. extend a hearty welcome and make the new employee feel welcome
   B. have the man sit and wait for a while before seeing him so that the employee realizes how busy the custodian is
   C. warn him of stern disciplinary action if he is late or absent excessively
   D. tell him he probably will have difficulty doing the work so that he doesn't become overconfident

4. The one of the following subjects of a fire prevention training program which is MOST readily applied on the job is the   4.___

   A. elimination of fire hazards
   B. use of portable fire extinguishers
   C. knowledge of types of fires
   D. method of reporting fires

5. A custodian who is a good supervisor will NOT   5.___

   A. tell his men what their jobs are and why they are important
   B. show his men how their jobs are to be done in the right way
   C. require some of the men to do their jobs in the presence of the supervisor demonstrating that they understand the job
   D. leave his men alone because they will always do their jobs correctly once they have received their instructions

6. When a custodian sees a worker doing his job incorrectly, he should   6.___

   A. tell the worker to be more careful
   B. suspend the worker until he learns to do the job correctly
   C. tell the worker specifically how the job should be done
   D. scold the man

7. An employee who is a good worker but is often late for work 7._____

   A. is lazy and should be dismissed
   B. cannot tell time
   C. can have no excuse for being late more than once a month
   D. should be questioned by his supervisor to try to find out why he is late

8. When starting any disciplinary action, a custodian who is a good supervisor should 8._____

   A. show his annoyance by losing his temper
   B. be apologetic
   C. be sarcastic
   D. be firm and positive

9. The BEST way for a custodian to maintain good employee morale is to 9._____

   A. avoid praising any one employee
   B. always have an alibi for his own mistakes
   C. encourage cliques by giving them information before giving it to other workers
   D. give adequate credit and praise when due

10. The BEST way for a custodian to tell if the night cleaners have done their work well is to check 10._____

    A. on how much cleaning material has been used
    B. on how much waste paper was collected
    C. the building for cleanliness
    D. the floor mops to see if they are still wet

11. The one of the following which is the BEST reason for introducing a training program is that the 11._____

    A. quality of work is above standard
    B. employees are all experienced
    C. accident rate is too high
    D. complaints are negligible

12. The FIRST step in training an inexperienced individual in a particular job is to 12._____

    A. put him to work and watch for mistakes
    B. put him to work and tell him to call for help if he needs it
    C. put him at ease and then find out what he knows about the work
    D. tell him to watch the least experienced worker on the job because the training is still fresh in his mind

13. As used in job analysis, the term *job breakdown* means 13._____

    A. any equipment failure
    B. any failure on the part of the worker to complete the job
    C. dividing the job into a series of steps
    D. reducing the number of workers by 50 percent

14. In dealing with the public, a custodian should be

    A. indulgent
    B. courteous
    C. disagreeable
    D. unavailable

15. If a custodian sees a group of people in front of his building preparing to form a picket line, he should

    A. turn on a lawn sprinkler to spray the pickets
    B. order the pickets off the sidewalk in front of the building
    C. show the pickets he is sympathetic with their complaint against the city
    D. contact his supervisor immediately for instructions

16. When electric service in a public building is to be shut off from 10 A.M. Tuesday to 11:30 the next morning because a new electric feeder cable is being installed, the custodian should

    A. prepare a memo to all office supervisors in the building, notifying them of the situation, and deliver a copy to each office as soon as possible
    B. prepare a notice of the impending power stoppage and post it in the lobby early Tuesday morning
    C. tell the electrical contractor to notify the tenants when he is about to shut off the power
    D. discontinue elevator service at 10 A.M. on Tuesday as an indication to the tenants that the power supply is off

17. Time standards for cleaning are of value ONLY if

    A. a bonus is promised if the time standards are beaten
    B. the cleaners determine the methods and procedures to be used
    C. accompanied by a completely detailed description of the methods to be used
    D. a schematic diagram of the area is made available to the cleaners

18. Of the following, the one which is the LEAST important factor in deciding that additional training is necessary for the men you supervise is that

    A. the quality of work is below standard
    B. supplies are being wasted
    C. too much time is required to do specific jobs
    D. the absentee rate has declined

19. To promote proper safety practices in the operation of power tools and equipment, the custodian should emphasize in meetings with his staff that

    A. every accident can be prevented through proper safety regulations
    B. proper safety practices will probably make future safety meetings unnecessary
    C. when safety rules are followed, tools and equipment will work better
    D. safety rules are based on past experience with the best methods of preventing accidents

20. As a custodian, a GOOD practical method to use in determining whether an employee is doing his job properly is to

    A. assume that if he asks no questions, he knows the work
    B. question him directly on details of the job
    C. inspect and follow-up the work which is assigned to him
    D. ask other employees how this employee is making out

21. If an employee continually asks how he should do his work, the custodian should

    A. dismiss him immediately
    B. pretend he does not hear him unless he persists
    C. explain the work carefully but encourage him to use his own judgment
    D. tell him not to ask so many questions

22. As a custodian, you have instructed an employee to wet mop a certain area.
    To be sure that the employee understands the instructions you have given him, you should

    A. ask him to repeat the instructions to you
    B. check with him after he has done the job
    C. watch him while he is doing the job
    D. repeat the instructions to the employee

23. As a custodian, one of your men disagrees with your evaluation of his work.
    Of the following, the BEST way to handle this situation would be to

    A. explain that you are in a better position to evaluate his work than he is
    B. tell him that since the other men are satisfied with your evaluation, he should accept their opinions
    C. explain the basis of your evaluation and discuss it with him
    D. refuse to discuss his complaint in order to maintain discipline

24. Of the following, the one which is NOT a purpose of a cleaning job breakdown is to

    A. eliminate unnecessary steps
    B. determine the type of floor wax to use
    C. rearrange the sequence of operations to save time
    D. combine steps or actions where practicable

25. The BEST method of making cleaning assignments in a large building is by means of

    A. daily rotation
    B. specific assignment
    C. individual choice
    D. chronological order

KEY (CORRECT ANSWERS)

1.	C	11.	C
2.	C	12.	C
3.	A	13.	C
4.	A	14.	B
5.	D	15.	D
6.	C	16.	A
7.	D	17.	C
8.	D	18.	D
9.	D	19.	D
10.	C	20.	C

21. C
22. A
23. C
24. B
25. B

READING COMPREHENSION
UNDERSTANDING AND INTERPRETING WRITTEN MATERIAL

EXAMINATION SECTION
TEST 1

DIRECTIONS: Each question or incomplete statement is followed by several suggested answers or completions. Select the one that BEST answers the question or completes the statement. *PRINT THE LETTER OF THE CORRECT ANSWER IN THE SPACE AT THE RIGHT.*

Questions 1-3.

DIRECTIONS: Questions 1 through 3 are to be answered in accordance with the following passage.

Terrazzo flooring will last a very long time if it is cared for properly. Lacquers, shellac, or varnish preparations should never be used on terrazzo. Soap cleaners are not recommended since they dull the appearance of the floor. Alkaline solutions are harmful, so a neutral cleaner or non-alkaline synthetic detergents will give best results. If the floor is very dirty, it may be necessary to scrub it. The same neutral cleaning solution should be used for scrubbing as for mopping. Scouring powder may be sprinkled at particularly dirty spots. Do not use steel wool for scrubbing. Small pieces of steel filings left on the floor will rust and dis-color the terrazzo. Non-woven nylon or open-mesh fabric abrasive pads are suitable for scrubbing terrazzo floors.

1. According to the passage above, the BEST cleaning agent for terrazzo flooring is a(n)   1.____
   A. soap cleaner   B. varnish preparation
   C. neutral cleaner   D. alkaline solution

2. According to the passage above, terrazzo floors should NOT be scrubbed with   2.____
   A. non-woven nylon abrasive pads
   B. steel wool
   C. open-mesh fabric abrasive pads
   D. scouring powder

3. As used in the passage above, the word *discolor* means MOST NEARLY   3.____
   A. crack   B. scratch   C. dissolve   D. stain

Questions 4-7.

DIRECTIONS: Questions 4 through 7 are to be answered in accordance with the information given in the following passage.

MOPPING FLOORS

When mopping hardened cement floors, either painted or unpainted, a soap and water mixture should be used. This should be made by dissolving half a cup of soft soap in a pail of hot water. It is not desirable, however, under any circumstances, to use a soap and water mixture on cement floors that are not hardened. For mopping this type of floor, it is recommended that the cleaning agent be made up of 2 ounces of laundry soda mixed in a pail of water.

Soaps are not generally used on hard tile floors because slippery films may build up on the floor. It is generally recommended that these floors be mopped using a pail of hot water in which has been mixed 2 ounces of washing powder for each gallon of water. The floors should then be rinsed thoroughly.

After the mopping is finished, proper care should be taken of the mop. This is done by first cleaning the mop in clear warm water. Then, it should be wrung out, after which the strands of the mop should be untangled. Finally, the mop should be hung by its handle to dry.

4. According to the above passage, you should NEVER use a soap and water mixture when mopping _____ floors.

   A. hardened cement
   B. painted
   C. unhardened cement
   D. unpainted

5. According to the above passage, using laundry soda mixed in a pail of water as a cleaning agent is recommended for

   A. all floors
   B. all floors except hard tile floors
   C. some cement floors
   D. linoleum floor coverings *only*

6. According to the above passage, the GENERALLY recommended mixture for mopping hard tile floors is _____ of hot water.

   A. 1/2 cup of soft soap for each gallon
   B. 1/2 cup of soft soap in a pail
   C. 2 ounces of washing powder in a pail
   D. 2 ounces of washing powder for each gallon

7. According to the above passage, the PROPER care of a mop after it is used includes

   A. cleaning it in clear cold water and hanging it by its handle to dry
   B. wringing it out, untangling and drying it
   C. untangling its strands before wringing it out
   D. untangling its strands while cleaning it in clear water

Questions 8-15.

DIRECTIONS: Questions 8 through 15 are to be answered ONLY in accordance with the following paragraph.

Many custodial foremen have discovered through experience that there are economies to be *realized* by using discretion when ordering items which are similar to each other. For example, it may be cheaper to order a *Sponge block, cellulose, WET SIZE: 6 in. x 4 3/4 in. x APPROXIMATELY 34 inches long* at $7.00 than it is to order separate *Sponges, cellulose, wet size: 2 in. x 4 in. x 6 in.* at 60¢. It does not pay to *over-order* on floor wax which may turn sour if not used soon enough. An average size college building cannot afford to have extra 30-inch floor brooms costing $19.75 each stored *on the shelf* for a couple of years or to let moths destroy the hair in such brooms if proper safeguards are not used.

8. According to the above passage, the items mentioned which are *similar* are

    A. floor brooms
    B. sponges
    C. floor waxes
    D. moths

9. As used in the above paragraph, the term *over-order* means to

    A. order again
    B. back order
    C. order too little
    D. order too much

10. Of the items for which prices are given in the above paragraph, the MOST expensive one is the

    A. 30-inch floor broom
    B. 6 in. x 4 3/4 in. x 34 in. sponge block
    C. 2 in. x 4 in. x 6 in. sponge
    D. floor wax

11. As used in the above paragraph, the word *realized* means MOST NEARLY

    A. obtained   B. lost   C. equalized   D. cheapened

12. According to the above paragraph, the one of the following which may be damaged by moths is the

    A. floor broom
    B. sponge
    C. cellulose
    D. wool cloth

13. As used in the above paragraph, the term *wet size* means

    A. the chemical treatment given to sponges
    B. the amount of water the sponge can hold
    C. that the sponges must be kept moist at all times
    D. that the measurements given were taken when the sponges were wet

14. As used in the above paragraph, the word *at* means

    A. near   B. arrived   C. each   D. new

15. As used in the above paragraph, the word *approximately* means

    A. exactly   B. about   C. economical   D. tan

Questions 16-17.

DIRECTIONS: Questions 16 and 17 are to be answered in accordance with the following paragraph.

Painting is done to preserve surfaces; and unless the surface is properly prepared, good preservation will not be possible. Apply paint only to clean dry surfaces. After a surface has been scaled, which means that all loose paint and rust are removed by chipping, scraping, and wire brushing, be sure all dust and dirt are completely removed.

16. According to the above paragraph, the MAIN purpose of painting a wall is to _____ the wall.   16._____

    A. clean
    B. waterproof
    C. protect
    D. remove dust from

17. According to the above paragraph,   17._____

    A. chipping, scraping, and wire brushing are the only methods permitted for cleaning surfaces
    B. painting is effective only when the surface is clean
    C. scaling refers only to the removal of rust
    D. paint may be applied on wet surfaces

Questions 18-21.

DIRECTIONS: Questions 18 through 21 are to be answered SOLELY on the basis of the following paragraph.

All cleaning agents and supplies should be kept in a central storeroom which should be kept locked and only the custodian, store-keeper, and foreman should have keys. Shelving should be provided for the smaller items while barrels containing scouring powder or other bulk material should be set on the floor or on special cradles. Each compartment in the shelves should be marked plainly and only the item indicated stored therein. Each barrel should also be marked plainly. It may also be desirable to keep special items such as electric lamps, flashlight batteries, etc. in a locked cabinet or separate room to which only the custodian and the night building foreman have keys.

18. According to the above paragraph, scouring powder   18._____

    A. should be kept on shelves
    B. comes in one-pound cans
    C. should be kept in a locked cabinet
    D. is a bulk material

19. According to the above paragraph,   19._____

    A. the storekeeper should not be entrusted with the safekeeping of light bulbs
    B. flashlight batteries should be stored in barrels
    C. the central storeroom should be kept locked
    D. only special items should be stored under lock and key

20. According to the above paragraph,   20._____

    A. each shelf compartment should contain at least four different items
    B. barrels must be stored in cradles
    C. all items stored should be in marked compartments
    D. crates of light bulbs should be stored in cradles

21. As used in the above paragraph, the word *cradle* means a 21.____

    A. dolly
    B. support
    C. doll's bed
    D. hand truck

Questions 22-25.

DIRECTIONS: Questions 22 through 25 are to be answered SOLELY on the basis of the following paragraph.

There are on the market many cleaning agents for which amazing claims are made. Chemical analysis shows that the majority of them are well-known chemicals slightly modified and packaged and sold under various trade names. For that reason, the agents which have been selected for your use are those whose cleaning properties are well-known and whose use can be standardized. It is obviously undesirable to offer too wide a selection as that would be confusing to the cleaner, but a sufficient number must be provided so that a satisfactory agent is available for each task.

22. According to the above paragraph, 22.____

    A. there are few cleaning agents on the market
    B. there are no really good cleaning agents on the market
    C. cleaning agents are sold under several different brand names
    D. all cleaning agents are the same

23. According to the above paragraph, 23.____

    A. all cleaning agents should be chemically analyzed before use
    B. the best cleaning agents are those for which no claims are made by the manufacturer
    C. different cleaning agents may be needed for different tasks
    D. all cleaning agents have been standardized by the federal government

24. As used in the above paragraph, the word *amazing* means 24.____

    A. illegal
    B. untrue
    C. astonishing
    D. specific

25. As used in the above paragraph, the word *modified* means 25.____

    A. changed   B. refined   C. labelled   D. diluted

KEY (CORRECT ANSWERS)

1. C
2. B
3. D
4. C
5. C

6. D
7. B
8. B
9. D
10. A

11. A
12. A
13. D
14. C
15. B

16. C
17. B
18. D
19. C
20. C

21. B
22. C
23. C
24. C
25. A

TEST 2

Questions 1-3.

DIRECTIONS: Questions 1 through 3 are to be answered in accordance with the following passage. Each question or incomplete statement is followed by several suggested answers or completions. Select the one that BEST answers the question or completes the statement. *PRINT THE LETTER OF THE CORRECT ANSWER IN THE SPACE AT THE RIGHT.*

    The method of cleaning which should generally be used is the space assignment method. Under this method, the buildings to be cleaned are divided into different sections. Within each section, each crew of Custodial Assistants is assigned to do one particular cleaning job. For example, within a section, one crew may be assigned to cleaning offices, another to scrubbing floors, a third to collecting trash, and so on. Other methods which may be used are the post assignment method and the gang cleaning method. Under the post assignment method, a Custodial Assistant is assigned to one area of a building and performs all cleaning jobs in that area. This method is seldom used except where buildings are so small and distant from each other that it is not economical to use the space assignment method. Under the gang cleaning method, a Custodial Foreman takes a number of Custodial Assistants through a section of the building. These Custodial Assistants work as a group and complete the various cleaning jobs as they go. This method is generally used only where the building contains very large open areas.

1. According to the passage above, under the space assignment method, each crew GENERALLY 1.____

    A. works as a group and does a variety of different cleaning jobs
    B. is assigned to one area and performs all cleaning jobs in that area
    C. does one particular cleaning job within a section of a building
    D. follows the Custodial Foreman through a building containing large, open areas

2. According to the passage above, the post assignment method is used MOSTLY where the buildings to be cleaned are _____ in size and situated _____. 2.____

    A. large; close together   B. small; close together
    C. large; far apart   D. small; far apart

3. As used in the passage above, the word *economical* means MOST NEARLY 3.____

    A. thrifty   B. agreed   C. unusual   D. wasteful

Questions 4-25.

DIRECTIONS: Each question consists of a statement. You are to indicate whether the statement is TRUE (T) or FALSE (F). *PRINT THE LETTER OF THE CORRECT ANSWER IN THE SPACE AT THE RIGHT.*

Questions 4-8.

DIRECTIONS: Questions 4 through 8 are to be answered in accordance with the information given in the following paragraph.

The removal of fine, loose dirt or dust from desks, chairs, filing cabinets, tables, and other furniture or office machines is called dusting. A yard of clean soft cloth, folded into a pad about nine inches square, is best for dusting. The cloth should be dry since oil or water on the cloth may streak the surface that is being dusted. When dusting a desk, care must be taken to put back in the same place any papers that were lifted or moved to one side. Thorough dusting of an office is important in order for the office to look neat and for the health of the people who work in that office.

4. The removal of fine, loose dirt or dust from furniture or office machines is called dusting.   4._____

5. A pad of cloth twelve inches square is best for dusting.   5._____

6. A dry cloth will streak the surface that is being dusted.   6._____

7. Papers that have been lifted or moved to one side when dusting a desk should be put back in the same place.   7._____

8. It is not important to dust an office thoroughly.   8._____

Questions 9-18.

DIRECTIONS: Questions 9 through 18 are to be answered in accordance with the information given in the following paragraphs.

WASHING OF WALLS

The washing of walls is important since wall-cleaning costs are an expensive item in the operating cost of building maintenance.

There is a right and a wrong way to wash walls. Streaks may be caused by water running down the dry wall below the place where one is working. This can be prevented by first wetting a section of the wall with water, starting at the bottom and working up before starting the actual washing operation with cleaning solution. Then, if the water runs down the wet wall, there will be almost no streaking. While washing a wall, the temperature should be reasonably low so that the water will not dry on the wall and cause streaks. Once the dirt on the wall is moistened, the wall must be kept wet until the dirt is removed. The washing of walls should be done with good sponges. One sponge should be for cleaning on the dirty wall and one for rinsing.

When working with the cleaning solution, start at the top of the wall and use a circular motion of the sponge and hand. Work across a given section first to the right and then to the left, and so on down to the base.

After the dirt has been removed, take clean, cool water and a clean sponge and go over the wall to be sure that it is perfectly clean and that no traces of the cleaning solution remain on the wall. Even clean water drying unevenly on a wall will cause slight streaks which become noticeable on the walls.

9. The amount of money spent to wash walls is a very small part in the expenses of running a building.   9._____

10. To prevent streaks when washing a wall, an employee should FIRST wet the wall, starting at the top and working down to the base of a wall.

10._____

11. If a wall is wet in the right way, there will be practically no streaks caused by water running down the wet wall.

11._____

12. If the walls are washed when the room is hot, streaks can be caused by water drying too quickly.

12._____

13. Once a dirty wall is made wet with water, it should be dried completely before the dirt is removed.

13._____

14. To wash walls properly, an employee should use at least two good sponges.

14._____

15. When washing with the cleaning solution, start at the bottom of the wall and work to the top, using a circular motion of the hand and sponge.

15._____

16. When washing with the cleaning solution, the CORRECT method is to work across each part of the wall going first to the left and ending on the right.

16._____

17. After the wall has been washed with the cleaning solution, it must be gone over again with clean water to remove any solution which is left on the wall.

17._____

18. When clean water is used to wash a wall, streaks will never appear, even if the wall dries unevenly.

18._____

Questions 19-25.

DIRECTIONS: Questions 19 through 25 are to be answered in accordance with the information given in the following passage.

CLEANING ELECTRIC LIGHT FIXTURES

A room may be dark not because there are not enough light fixtures but because the globes are dirty. As frequently as found necessary, and at least once a year, each globe on a light fixture should be taken down and carefully washed. It should be cleaned by using a solution of warm water to which has been added about two tablespoons full of washing soda for each 10 quarts of water. The globe must be thoroughly dried before it is put back or it is liable to crack from the heat of the lamp. At the time the globe is washed, the metal parts of the fixture should be wiped with a rag dampened in plain warm water. Most metal fixtures have been lacquered, and any cleaning solution would tend to destroy the lacquer. The electric light bulb should be unscrewed from the fixture and wiped with a slighly damp cloth. If it is burned out, it should be replaced at this time.

19. Dirty light globes will reduce the amount of light in a room.

19._____

20. Light globes should be cleaned only when the attendant replaces a burned out light bulb in a fixture.

20._____

21. To clean light globes, a solution of cold water and ordinary household ammonia should be used.

21._____

22. If a light globe is not completely dry when it is put back on a fixture after washing, the heat from the light bulb can break the globe. 22.____

23. The metal parts of a light fixture should be cleaned by using a dry rag to which has been added a few drops of a cleaning solution. 23.____

24. Most metal light fixtures have a coating of lacquer on them. 24.____

25. To clean a light bulb in a fixture, it should be unscrewed and wiped with a damp cloth. 25.____

KEY (CORRECT ANSWERS)

1.	C	11.	T
2.	D	12.	T
3.	A	13.	F
4.	T	14.	T
5.	F	15.	F
6.	F	16.	F
7.	T	17.	T
8.	F	18.	F
9.	F	19.	T
10.	F	20.	F

21. F
22. T
23. F
24. T
25. T

ARITHMETICAL REASONING
EXAMINATION SECTION
TEST 1

DIRECTIONS: Each question or incomplete statement is followed by several suggested answers or completions. Select the one that BEST answers the question or completes the statement. *PRINT THE LETTER OF THE CORRECT ANSWER IN THE SPACE AT THE RIGHT.*

1. Assume that a room measures 12'6" x 11'4". Its area is MOST NEARLY _____ sq. ft.   1._____
   A. 138
   B. 139
   C. 140
   D. 142

2. The SMALLEST subdivision found on the ordinary six-foot wooden rule is   2._____
   A. 1/32"
   B. 1/16"
   C. 1/8"
   D. 1/4"

3. The sum of the following numbers, 6 1/4, 5 3/16, 7 1/2, 8 1/8, and 7 5/16, is   3._____
   A. 34 1/4
   B. 34 5/16
   C. 34 3/8
   D. 34 7/16

4. 92796 divided by 376 is MOST NEARLY   4._____
   A. 245
   B. 247
   C. 249
   D. 251

5. Assume that an inspector will average 8 inspections per day.
   The number of days it will take seven inspectors to complete a total of 1,344 inspections at the same average rate is   5._____
   A. 24
   B. 26
   C. 28
   D. 30

6. The MAXIMUM number of 3" x 5" pieces that can be cut from one sheet of 17" x 22" paper is   6._____
   A. 20
   B. 21
   C. 22
   D. 23

7. Suppose you are told to print a year's supply of a form. If 1,500 copies are used each month and the form is printed three up on an 8 1/2" x 14" sheet and cut to 4 1/2" x 8 1/2", how many 8 1/2" x 14" sheets are needed (disregarding waste)?   7._____
   A. 3,000
   B. 4,500
   C. 5,400
   D. 6,000

8. The MAXIMUM number of 4" x 5" pieces that can be cut from five 500-sheet packages of 16" x 21" paper is   8._____
   A. 30,000
   B. 40,000
   C. 50,000
   D. 60,000

9. The manager of the project has asked you to compute the cost of 175 feet of electric wire needed for an installation in the project community room. This wire is listed in the catalog in 1,000-foot coils, each coil weighing 32 pounds and costing $1.14 a pound.
   The cost of the wire to be used is MOST NEARLY   9._____
   A. $4.35
   B. $5.94
   C. $6.24
   D. $6.39

10. One section of a project containing 800 apartments was constructed at a cost of $116,000 per apartment. The two remaining sections of the project, containing 625 apartments each, are still to be built.
In order that the average construction cost per apartment for the entire project will not exceed $130,000, the cost per apartment in the two sections still to be built should be APPROXIMATELY

    A. $131,000   B. $135,000   C. $139,000   D. $140,000

11. A certain project contains 57 two-room apartments (for 2 persons), 305 three-room apartments (for 3 persons), 309 four-room apartments (for 4 persons), 104 five-room apartments (for 4 persons), 197 five-room apartments (for 5 persons), and 52 five-room apartments (for 6 persons).
The percentage of 4-person apartments in this project is between

    A. 10 and 19.9   B. 20 and 29.9
    C. 30 and 39.9   D. 40 and 49.9

12. Assume that each year the value of a certain project depreciates 2 1/2% of its original value.
At the end of the third year, its value, after depreciation, is $6,734,900. The original value was MOST NEARLY

    A. $7,252,000   B. $7,253,000
    C. $7,280,000   D. $7,290,000

13. A housing project with A apartments contains a total of R rooms. The total number of residents is N.
The number of residents per apartment is expressed by

    A. N/A   B. R/A   C. A/N   D. N/R

14. A unit of ten housing assistants has been assigned the job of interviewing 1,800 applicants. They are each able to do two interviews an hour. After the job is one-third done, an improvement in the procedure is put into effect which makes it possible to save 25% of the time.
The number of 7-hour days required for the entire job is MOST NEARLY

    A. 10   B. 11   C. 12   D. 13

15. Assume that 135,200 new applications were received in a certain year for the 9,500 apartments made available in new projects. In addition, 32,900 old applications were reviewed for eligibility for the new apartments. Of these, 49,300 new and 9,400 old applicants were found eligible.
The percentage of eligible applicants who will NOT receive an apartment is

    A. under 75%   B. between 75% and 80%
    C. between 80% and 85%   D. over 85%

16. A project tenant who is a cabdriver works on a commission basis, receiving 42 1/2% of the fares. In addition, his earnings from tips are valued at 29% of the commissions. If his average monthly fares equal $520, then his annual earnings are

    A. between $3,000 and $3,400   B. between $3,400 and $3,800
    C. between $3,800 and $4,200   D. over $4,200

17. A project tenant's earning record for the year is as follows: up to January 15, unemployed; continuously employed for the rest of the year; from Monday, January 16, $430 a week; from Monday, April 3, $390 a week; from Monday, October 2, $450 a week. This tenant's yearly income is MOST NEARLY

    A. $15,000   B. $17,500   C. $21,000   D. $22,500

17.____

18. In a certain city in 2000, the average cost for constructing one apartment of a public housing project was $127,500, an increase of 4% over 1999.
    The cost of constructing a project of 1,500 apartments in 2000 was more than in 1999 by an amount which is MOST NEARLY

    A. $6,000,000   B. $6,150,000
    C. $7,400,000   D. $7,650,000

18.____

Questions 19-20.

DIRECTIONS: Questions 19 and 20 are to be answered SOLELY on the basis of the following paragraph.

A housing development has 450 apartments. The average weekly rent is $134.50 per apartment. The average amount of subsidy money added to the average weekly rent (to meet the total operating costs) is $68.00. Since the time when the amount of the subsidy was determined, operating costs for the development have increased by $3,960.00 per week.

19. If the subsidy is increased by 6%, what INCREASE in the average weekly rental will be necessary to meet monthly operating costs?

    A. $3.40   B. $4.72
    C. $8.80   D. No increase

19.____

20. What is the NEW total weekly operating cost per apartment?

    A. $76.80   B. $143.30   C. $211.30   D. $242.10

20.____

21. In a certain housing project, the average income of tenant families is $19,400 per annum and the average rent per apartment is $360 per month.
    If the average income increases 12% in a year while the average rent of an apartment increases 15%, how much MORE money will the average family have in a year after paying rent?

    A. $677.60   B. $1,680.00   C. $2,241.60   D. $4,968.00

21.____

22. A certain housing project has 1,860 tenant families. It has two playgrounds, both rectangular in shape. One measures 104 feet by 45 feet; the other is 74 feet by 53 feet.
    The number of square feet of playground space per family in this project is MOST NEARLY

    A. 3   B. 5   C. 7   D. 9

22.____

23. A particular housing project has 1,460 occupied apartments. If there are 12 new tenants in January, 14 in February, and 16 in March, the turnover rate for the first quarter of the year is MOST NEARLY

    A. 2.9%   B. 3.2%   C. 3.5%   D. 3.8%

23._____

24. In 2009, the cost of refrigerator repairs and maintenance at a certain housing project was $2,700 more than in 2008, representing an increase of 18%. A further increase at the same rate is expected in 2010.
    The cost of refrigerator repairs and maintenance in 2010 will be MOST NEARLY

    A. $6,000   B. $10,000   C. $18,000   D. $21,000

24._____

25. If a tenant earns $31,680 a year and his rent is 25% of his annual income, the amount of rent he pays each month is

    A. $660   B. $690   C. $720   D. $810

25._____

KEY (CORRECT ANSWERS)

1. D		11. D	
2. B		12. C	
3. C		13. A	
4. B		14. B	
5. A		15. C	
6. B		16. B	
7. D		17. C	
8. B		18. C	
9. D		19. B	
10. C		20. C	

21. B
22. B
23. A
24. D
25. A

SOLUTIONS TO PROBLEMS

1. Area = (12.5')(11 1/3') = 141 2/3 sq.ft. ≈ 142 sq.ft.

2. 1/16" the smallest marking on a six-foot wooden ruler.

3. 6 1/4 + 5 3/16 + 7 1/2 + 8 1/8 + 7 5/16 = 33 22/16 = 34 3/8

4. 92,796 ÷ 376 ≈ 246.8 ≈ 247

5. 7 inspectors can do a total of 56 inspections per day. Then, 1344 ÷ 56 = 24 days

6.

7. Each year, (1500)(12) = 18,000 forms are needed. Since 3 forms can fit on each sheet, 18,000 ÷ 3 = 6000 sheets are needed.

8. 16" ÷ 4" = 4 and 21" ÷ 5" rounds down to 4. Then, (4)(4) = 16 pieces of dimensions 4"x5" can be cut from each original 16"x21" piece of paper. For 2500 original sheets, we can cut (2500)(16) = 40,000 4"x5" pieces.

9. Let x = weight of the 175-ft. wire. x/175 = 32/1000. Solving, x = 5.6 lbs. The cost of this wire = (5.6)($1.14) = $6.38

10. Let x = cost per apartment for the remaining 1250 apartments. Then, [(800)($116,000)+1250x]/2050 < $130,000. Simplifying, $92,800,000 + 1250x < $266,500,000. Solving, x < $138,960 or approx. $139,000.

11. (309+104) ÷ (57+305+309+104+197+52) = 413/1024 = 40.33%

12. .925x = 6,734,900; x = 7,280,000

13. If A apartments contain N residents, the number of residents per apartment = N/A

14. (10)(2) = 20 applicants can be interviewed in 1 hour. Then, 600 ÷ 20 = 30 hours. The remaining 1200 applicants would normally require an additional 1200 ÷ 20 = 60 hours; however, the new procedure of interviewing these 1200 applicants will take (60)(.75) = 45 hours. Total time for all 1800 applicants = 30 + 45 = 75 hours. Finally, 75 ÷ 7 = 10.7 ≈ 11 days. (using 7 hours = 1 day)

15. 49,300 + 9,400 = 58,700 eligible applicants. Since only 9500 apartments are available, 49,200 eligible applicants will not receive an apartment. Finally, 49,200 ÷ 58,700 = 83.8%.

16. If his monthly fare averages $520, he gets a commission of ($520)(.425) = $221 and tips of ($221)(.29) ~ $64. His annual earnings = (12)($221+$64) = $3420.

17. (11)($430) + (26)($390) + (13)($450) = $20,720 = $21,000

18. The cost for one apartment in 1999 was $127,500 * 1.04 = $122,596. The cost difference per apartment from 1999 to 2000 was ~ $4904. For 1500 apartments, the additional cost was (1500)($4904) = $7,356,000 ~ $7,400,000.

19. $3960 ÷ 450 = $8.80 required increase per apartment to meet new operating costs. The increase in the subsidy = (.06)($68) = $4.08. The weekly rental increase necessary = $8.80 - $4.08 = $4.72

20. New operating cost per apartment (weekly) = $134.50 + $68 + $8.80 = $211.30

21. $19,400 - (12)($360) = $15,080. The new annual income = ($19,400)(1.12) = $21,728 and the new monthly rent = ($360X1.15) = $414. Then, $21,728 - (12)($414) = $16,760. Finally, $16,760 - $15,080 = $1680

22. (104)(45) + (74)(53) = 8602 sq.ft. Then, 8602 ÷ 1860 ≈ 5

23. (12+14+16) ÷ 1460 = 42/1460 ≈ 2.9%

24. The cost in 2008 was $2700 ÷ .18 = $15,000. Thus, the cost in 2009 was $15,000 + 2700 = $17,700. Finally, the cost in 2010 was ($17,700X1.18) = $20,886 = $21,000

25. (.25)($31,680) = $7,920. Then, $7,920 12 = $660

TEST 2

DIRECTIONS: Each question or incomplete statement is followed by several suggested answers or completions. Select the one that BEST answers the question or completes the statement. *PRINT THE LETTER OF THE CORRECT ANSWER IN THE SPACE AT THE RIGHT.*

1. The area of the plot plan shown at the right is _____ square feet.
   A. 25,300
   B. 26,700
   C. 28,100
   D. 30,500

   (Plot dimensions: 270', 70', 150', 155', 115')

   1.____

2. A pump that removes 30 gallons of water per minute is pumping water from a cellar 30 feet x 50 feet covered with eight inches of water. One cubic foot of water equals 7.5 gallons of water.
   The number of minutes it will take to remove the eight inches of water from the cellar is

   A. 200   B. 225   C. 250   D. 275

   2.____

3. In order to clean an office with 20,000 sq.ft. of space in 4 hours using a standard of 900 sq.ft. per hour, the number of cleaners you should assign to do the job is MOST NEARLY

   A. 4   B. 6   C. 8   D. 10

   3.____

4. The area of a floor 35' wide and 45' long is, in square yards, MOST NEARLY

   A. 175   B. 262   C. 525   D. 1,575

   4.____

Questions 5-6.

DIRECTIONS: Questions 5 and 6 are to be answered on the basis of the following paragraph.

A tenant in a housing development receives a semi-monthly public assistance check of $468 and pays a monthly rental of $284 from the proceeds. The tenant is about to begin paying $36 additional per month toward total rent arrears of $544. At the same time that the arrears payments begin, his semi-monthly check increases to $484.

5. What will be the TOTAL change in monthly net income after all rent payments?

   A. $12   B. $8   C. $4   D. No change

   5.____

6. If, instead of paying only $36 per month toward the arrears, the total increase in public assistance payments is used to increase arrears payments, how many months will it take the tenant to pay off the arrears? _____ months.

   A. 8   B. 10   C. 12   D. 14

   6.____

7. A tenant is offered two options in renewing a lease:
   (1) a one-year lease at a 10% increase in rent, or
   (2) a three-year lease at an 18% increase in rent.
   The tenant's current rent is $220 monthly.
   If the tenant takes the first option and continues to live in the apartment for three years with a 10% increase in rent each year, what would be the DIFFERENCE between the total rent he would pay and the rent he would have paid had he chosen the three-year lease?

   A. $266.64   B. $276.64   C. $1,425.60   D. $1,692.24

8. A certain task that an assistant performs takes approximately 45 minutes per unit of work. Seventy-five percent of his work day is spent on this task.
   Assuming that he works seven hours per day, how many work days will it take him to finish 1,470 units of work?

   A. 153   B. 210   C. 240   D. 270

9. It takes 5 1/2 gallons of paint to paint an average apartment, and it requires 18 man hours.
   If the price of paint increases $2.40 per gallon and the pay of the painters increases $2.65 per hour, what is the INCREASE in the cost of painting an apartment?

   A. $49.90   B. $50.90   C. $59.90   D. $60.90

10. A government employee can process a certain type of report in 23 minutes.
    How many such reports could he finish processing in a work day from 9:00 A.M. to 5:00 P.M., with a 45-minute lunch break and two 10-minute coffee breaks?

    A. 16   B. 17   C. 18   D. 19

11. The income of a tenant family is as follows: The husband has a gross income of $280 per week; the wife has a gross income of $220 per week. Deductions from gross family income total $116 per week, plus an allowable child care expense of $56 per week.
    What is the net annual income of the family after deductions and allowable child care expenses?

    A. $16,656   B. $17,056   C. $18,656   D. $19,056

12. Assume that you receive the following bills and coins for use as a change fund: 180 twenty-dollar bills, 110 ten-dollar bills, 125 five-dollar bills, 100 one-dollar bills, 200 quarters, 125 dimes, 50 nickels, and 150 pennies. You cash checks for tenants out of this fund in the following amounts: $134.96, $83.84, $76.96, and $74.37.
    The BALANCE in the fund after paying out these amounts should be

    A. $4,096.37   B. $5,021.47   C. $5,121.37   D. $5,233.87

13. Suppose that a tenant has paid a rent of $312.80 per month for six months and the rent is then increased by 5%.
    After paying the increased rent for six months, how much MORE money has the tenant paid in rent than was paid in the previous six months?

    A. $15.64   B. $93.84   C. $112.56   D. $187.68

14. Assume that $13,965.31 was collected at a project on a Monday. If the collections at this project on Tuesday were 7% more than on Monday, then the Tuesday total was MOST NEARLY

    A. $12,987.74
    B. $14,492.90
    C. $14,942.88
    D. $14,977.57

15. Suppose that $12,864 was collected on a Thursday and $17,243 was collected on Friday.
    The percentage increase in Friday's collections over Thursday's collections was MOST NEARLY

    A. 25%
    B. 34%
    C. 66%
    D. 75%

16. If the total monthly rent roll at Project Y is $116,610 and the cash collections of current rent at the end of the first week of the month totaled 93% of the total monthly rent roll, then the amount of current rent still uncollected was

    A. $7,160.70
    B. $8,162.70
    C. $8,273.30
    D. $8,621.30

17. A city employee whose weekly pay was $432.60 for a 35-hour work week was required to work 7 hours overtime during one week. The employee asked what the pay rate was for this overtime and was informed that the first five hours would be paid at his regular hourly rate and the next two hours at one and one-half times his regular rate.
    According to this information, the total amount of pay for overtime worked by this employee during this week was

    A. $61.80
    B. $86.52
    C. $98.88
    D. $136.68

18. If 3/4 of a number is 10 more than 1/2 the number, the number is

    A. 8
    B. 20
    C. 40
    D. 50

19. Instead of dividing a number by 5, you can achieve the same result by

    A. multiplying by 1/2
    B. dividing by 1/2
    C. multiplying by .2
    D. dividing by .2

20. What percent of 4/5 is 7/10?

    A. 56%
    B. 87 1/2%
    C. 114 2/7%
    D. 178 4/7%

21. When a number is multiplied by three and then divided by 1/4, the net result is that the number is

    A. multiplied by 3/4
    B. multiplied by 4/3
    C. multiplied by 12
    D. divided by 12

22. Three tellers, all working at the same rate of speed, were able to post 1,260 rent charges in 14 hours.
    How long would the job have taken if only two of these tellers had been assigned? _____ hours.

    A. 7
    B. 9 1/3
    C. 18
    D. 21

23. A teller filed 440 ledger cards in an hour. If this amounted to 12 1/2% of the task, what was the TOTAL number of cards he was required to file?   23._____

    A. 360   B. 3,520   C. 3,600   D. 5,402

24. $5,470.80 is to be paid to 47 employees, each of whom will receive the same amount in cash.   24._____
If in making the payment you give each employee the minimum number of bills and coins possible, how many $1 bills will you need to meet the payroll?

    A. 47   B. 94   C. 188   D. 282

25. A commercial tenant pays an annual rental under a graduated percentage lease. The annual rental is based on gross sales for the year and is computed as follows: 25._____

    On the first $50,000 of gross sales   - 5%
    On the next $25,000   - 4 1/2%
    On the next $15,000   - 3 1/2%
    On the next $10,000   - 2 1/2%
    On sales in excess of $100,000   - 1 1/4%

His gross sales for the year were $116,292.80.
His rental for that year was MOST NEARLY

    A. $2,703.60   B. $4,603.60
    C. $5,203.60   D. $11,453.60

KEY (CORRECT ANSWERS)

1. C	11. B
2. C	12. C
3. B	13. B
4. A	14. C
5. C	15. B
6. A	16. B
7. A	17. C
8. B	18. C
9. D	19. C
10. C	20. B

21. C
22. D
23. B
24. A
25. B

SOLUTIONS TO PROBLEMS

1. Using a horizontal dotted line, we construct two rectangles. Total area = (270')(70') + (115')(150'-70') = 28,100 sq.ft.

2. (30')(50')(2/3') = 1000 cu.ft., which contains (1000)(7.5) = 7500 gallons. Then, 7500 ÷ 30 = 250 minutes

3. 20,000 ÷ 900 = 22.$\bar{2}$ man-hours. To complete the job in 4 hours, use 22.2 ÷ 4 ≈ 6 cleaners.

4. (35')(45') = 1575 sq.ft. Then, 1575 ÷ 9 = 175 sq.yds.

5. ($468)(2) - $284 = $652 net income. With changes, ($484)(2) -$320 = $648 new net income. Monthly net income = $4

6. ($484)(2) - ($468)(2) = $32. Then, $32 + $36 = $68. Finally, $544 ÷ $68 = 8 months.

7.
```
Yr. 1: $242 x 12 =          2904.00
Yr. 2: + 10% + $290.40 =    3194.40
Yr. 3: + 10% + $310.44 =    3573.84
                            9612.24
```
9612.24 9612.24 - 9345.60 = $266.64

8. (.75)(7) = 5.25 hrs. assigned to this task per day. 1470 units of work will require (1470)(45) = 66,150 min. Since he has 5.25 hours = 315 min. each day, the number of days needed = 66,150 ÷ 315 = 210.

9. Change in cost = ($2.40)(5.5) + ($2.65)(18) = $60.90

10. From 9:00 AM to 5:00 PM is 8 hours. Then, 480 - 45 - (2)(10) = 415 min. Finally, 415 ÷ 23 = 18

11. $280 + $220 - $116 - $56 = $328. Then, ($328)(52) = $17,056 annually.

12. (180)($20) + (110)($10) + (125)($5) + (100)($1) + (200)($0.25) + (125)($0.10) + (50)($0.05) + (150)($0.01) - $134.96 - $83.84 - $76.96 - $74.37 = $5121.37

13. ($312.80)(6) = $1876.80. With the 5% increase, (312.80)(1.05)(6) = $1970.64. The additional cost = $93.84

14. ($13,965.31)(1.07) = $14,942.88

15. $17,243 - $12,864 = $4379. Then, $\frac{\$4379}{\$12,864} \approx 34\%$

16. Amount uncollected = (.07)($116,610) = $8162.70

17. $432.60 ÷ 35 = $12.36 per hour on regular pay. His overtime pay per hour = ($12.36)(1.5) = $18.54. His pay for extra time = (5)($12.36) + (2)($18.54) = $98.88.

18. Let x = missing number. Then, 3/4 x = 10 + 1/2 x. Simplifying, 1/4 x = 10. Solving, x = 40

19. Dividing by 5 is equivalent to multiplying by 1/5 = .2

20. $\dfrac{7}{10} \div \dfrac{4}{5} = \dfrac{7}{10} \cdot \dfrac{5}{4} = \dfrac{7}{8} = 87.5\%$

21. Since dividing by 1/4 means multiplying by 4, the net result for the given statement is multiplying by (3)(4) = 12

22. (3)(14) = 42 worker-hours. Then, 42 ÷ 2 = 21 hours

23. 440 ÷ .125 = 3520 ledger cards

24. $5470.80 ÷ 47 = $116.40. By using the minimum number of bills, each employee would receive one $1 bill toward the $116.40. Thus, for 47 employees, 47 $1 bills would be needed.

25. Total rental - (.05)($50,000) + (.045)($25,000) + (.035)($15,000) + (.025)($10,000) + (.0125X16,292.80) = $4603.66 ≈ $4603.60

TEST 3

DIRECTIONS: Each question or incomplete statement is followed by several suggested answers or completions. Select the one that BEST answers the question or completes the statement. *PRINT THE LETTER OF THE CORRECT ANSWER IN THE SPACE AT THE RIGHT.*

1. 1/6 is the same as

    A. .16 2/3%   B. 16 2/3%   C. .165   D. 16 2/3

2. 205% written as a decimal is

    A. .0205   B. .205   C. 2.05   D. 20.5

3. The sum of the fractions 2/3, 2/4, 5/6, and 7/8 is

    A. 1 15/16   B. 2 1/4   C. 2 3/4   D. 2 7/8

4. 24 3/8 multiplied by 48 amounts to

    A. 1,115   B. 1,121   C. 1,160   D. 1,170

5. One hundred pennies weigh 15 oz.
   The value of 4 lbs., 5 oz. of pennies is

    A. $4.33   B. $4.50   C. $4.60   D. $5.13

6. Which of the following is GREATER than .5?

    A. 1/8   B. 5/9   C. 5.5%   D. 20%

7. A recreation leader and his assistant arranged a picnic in the country for a group of 20 project tenants. Five tenants went in the leader's car and five went in the assistant's car, each tenant paying his driver $1.30 for the roundtrip. The ten tenants who went by bus paid $2.50 for the roundtrip. It was agreed that the tenants who went by car would each pay an additional amount which would be distributed to the tenants who went by bus so that all the tenants would pay the same amount for transportation.
   What ADDITIONAL amount would a tenant who went by car pay?

    A. 60¢   B. 70¢   C. 90¢   D. $1.20

8. An employee whose normal work day was 7 hours was required to work overtime, for which he took compensatory time off on an hour-for-hour basis in lieu of overtime pay. In a month with 21 working days, he worked as follows:
   First week - worked overtime 5 1/2 hours and took off 4 1/4 hours
   Second week - worked overtime 10 hours and took off 10 1/2 hours
   Third week - took one vacation day
   Balance of month - worked regular schedule
   How many hours did he work during the month?

    A. 129 3/4   B. 135 1/4   C. 139 3/4   D. 140 3/4

9. Suppose that you have received the following bills and coins for use as a change fund: 230 twenty-dollar bills, 130 ten-dollar bills, 175 five-dollar bills, 150 one-dollar bills, 220 quarters, 150 dimes, 60 nickels, and 200 pennies. You cash checks for tenants out of this fund in the following amounts: $120.75, $95.57, $75.40, and $48.50.
   The balance of cash in the fund after paying out these amounts SHOULD be

   A. $5,159.88   B. $5,659.78   C. $6,649.88   D. $6,659.78

10. A caretaker received $350 for having worked from Monday through Friday, 9 A.M. to 5 P.M. with one hour a day for lunch.
    The number of hours the caretaker would have to work to earn $60 is

    A. 10
    B. 6
    C. 70 divided by 12
    D. 70 minus 12

11. If the cost of a broom went up from $8.00 to $12.00, the percent INCREASE in the original cost is

    A. A. 20   B. 25   C. 33 1/3   D. 50

12. The AVERAGE of the numbers 3, 5, 7, 8, 12 is

    A. 5   B. 6   C. 7   D. 8

13. The cost of 100 bags of cotton cleaning cloths, 89 pounds per bag, at 70 cents per pound, is

    A. $5,493.50   B. $6,230.00   C. $7,000.00   D. $8,900.00

14. If 5 1/2 bags of sweeping compound cost $55.00, then 6 1/2 bags would cost

    A. $60.00   B. $62.50   C. $65.00   D. $67.50

15. The cost of cleaning supplies in a project averaged $3,300 a month during the first 8 months of the year.
    How much can be spent each month for the last four months if the total amount that can be spent for cleaning supplies for the year is $38,800?

    A. $1,240   B. $2,200   C. $3,100   D. $3,300

16. A shelf in a supply closet can safely hold only 100 pounds. A package of paper towels weighs 2 pounds, a carton of disinfectant weighs 8 pounds, and a box of soap weighs 1 pound. There are already 6 cartons of disinfectant and 6 boxes of soap on the shelf. How many packages of towels can be SAFELY placed there?

    A. 20   B. 23   C. 25   D. 27

17. A cleaning solution is made up of 4 gallons of water, 1 pint of liquid soap, and 1 pint of ammonia.
    How many gallons of water are needed to use up a gallon of ammonia?
    _____ gallons.

    A. 8   B. 16   C. 24   D. 32

18. Suppose a caretaker has 50 stair halls to clean.
    If he cleans 74% of them, the number of stair halls still UNCLEANED is

    A. 38   B. 26   C. 24   D. 13

19. If a man has a 12-foot piece of wood and wishes to cut it into two pieces so that one piece is twice as long as the other, the LONGER piece should be _____ feet. 19.____

   A. 7   B. 7 1/2   C. 8   D. 8 1/2

20. A city employee, whose weekly salary is $537.60 for a 35-hour workweek, was required to work 7 hours overtime during one week. The employee asked what the pay rate was for this overtime and was informed that he would be paid for the first five hours at his regular hourly rate and the next two hours at one and one-half times his regular hourly rate. According to this information, the GROSS pay for overtime worked by this employee during this week was 20.____

   A. $76.80   B. $107.52   C. $122.88   D. $161.28

21. Assume that you receive the following bills and coins for use as a change fund: 120 twenty-dollar bills, 150 ten-dollar bills, 100 five-dollar bills, 100 one-dollar bills, 100 quarters, 50 dimes, 25 nickels, and 200 pennies. You cash checks for tenants out of this fund in the following amounts: $189.30, $87.16, $72.90, and $68.50.
   The cash balance in the fund after cashing these checks should be 21.____

   A. $4,115.39   B. $4,325.01
   C. $4,713.09   D. $4,951.11

22. If the total monthly rent roll at Project X is $121,990 and the cash collections of current rent at the end of the first week of the month were 95% of the total monthly rent roll, then the amount of current rent still uncollected was 22.____

   A. $5,679.90   B. $6,099.50
   C. $6,211.90   D. $6,312.50

23. Suppose that a tenant has paid $172.40 per month in rent for six months and the rent is then increased by 5%. After paying the increased rent for six months, how much MORE money has the tenant paid in rent than was paid in the previous six months? 23.____

   A. $8.62   B. $51.72   C. $57.52   D. $60.58

24. The rents for three families in a relocation site come to a total of $9,720 per year. If Family A pays $3,480 per year and Family B pays $2,400 per year, how much does Family C pay? 24.____

   A. $2,760   B. $3,840   C. $4,200   D. $5,800

25. In a certain project, an exterminator is told to spray 120 apartments, 40 apartments, 20 basements, 80 apartments, 50 storerooms, and 10 compactors.
   The TOTAL number of apartments which should be sprayed is 25.____

   A. 240   B. 260   C. 310   D. 320

KEY (CORRECT ANSWERS)

1.	B	11.	D
2.	C	12.	C
3.	D	13.	B
4.	D	14.	C
5.	C	15.	C
6.	B	16.	B
7.	A	17.	D
8.	D	18.	D
9.	D	19.	C
10.	B	20.	C

21. A
22. B
23. B
24. B
25. A

SOLUTIONS TO PROBLEMS

1. $\dfrac{1}{6} = .1\overline{6} = 16\dfrac{2}{3}\%$

2. 205% = 2.05

3. 2/3 + 2/4 + 5/6 + 7/8 = 69/24 = 2 7/8

4. (24 3/8)(48) = (24.375)(48) = 1170

5. 4 lbs. 5 oz. = 69 oz. Let x = required weight. Then, $\dfrac{\$1.00}{15} = \dfrac{x}{69}$ Solving, x = $4.60

6. $\dfrac{5}{9} = .\overline{5} > .5$

7. The total paid by all 20 tenants was (10)($1.30) + (10)($2.50) = $38.00. If each person had paid the same amount, it would be $38.00 ÷ 20 = $1.90. So, the additional amount owed by each tenant who went by car was $0.60.

8. 1st week: 35 + 5 1/2 - 4 1/4 = 36 1/4 hrs. 2nd week: 35 + 10 - 10 1/2 = 34 1/2 hrs. 3rd week: (7)(4) = 28 hrs. Balance of month: (7)(21-15) = 42 hrs. Total hrs. = 140 3/4

9. (230)($20) + (130)($10) + (175)($5) + (150)($1) + (220)(.25) + (150)(.10) + (60)(.05) + (200)(.01) - $120.75 - $95.57 - $75.40 - $48.50 = $6659.78

10. 9 AM to 5 PM minus 1 hour for lunch = 35 hrs./wk. x = required number of hrs. Then, $\dfrac{\$350}{35} = \dfrac{\$60}{x}$. Solving, x = 6

11. ($12.00 - $8.00) ÷ $8.00 = 4 = 50%

12. (3+5+7+8+12) ÷ 5 = 35 ÷ 5 = 7

13. (89)(100) = 8900 lbs. Then, (8900)($0.70) = $6230.00

14. Let x = cost. $\dfrac{5.5}{\$55} = \dfrac{6.5}{x}$. Solving, x = $65.00

15. $38,800 - (8)($3300) = $12,400. Then, $12,400 ÷ 4 = $3100

16. (6)(8) + (6)(1) = 54 lbs. Only 100 - 54 = 46 more pounds can be placed on the shelf. Finally, 46 ÷ 2 = 23 pkgs. of towels.

17. Since 8 pints = 1 gallon, a gallon of ammonia requires (8)(4) = 32 gallons of water.

18. (50)(.26) = 13 halls uncleaned

19. Let x = longer piece and 1/2 x = shorter piece. Then, x + 1/2 x = 12 So, 3/2 x = 12, and x = 8 feet

20. $537.60 ÷ 35 = $15.36 per hour for regular pay. Overtime pay per hour = (15.36)(1.5) = $23.04. His overtime pay = (5)($15.36) + (2)($23.04) = $122.88

21. (120)($20) + (150)($10) + (100)($5) + (100)($1) + (100)($0.25) + (50)($0.10) + (25)($0.05) + (200)($0.01) - $189.30 - $87.16 - $72.90 - $68.50 = $4115.39.

22. ($121,990)(.05) = $6099.50 uncollected

23. ($172.40)(1.05) = 181.02. Then, ($181.02)(6) - ($172.40)(6) = $51.72

24. Family C pays $9720 - $3480 - $2400 = $3840

25. 120 + 40 + 80 = 240 apartments

SUPERVISION STUDY GUIDE

Social science has developed information about groups and leadership in general and supervisor-employee relationships in particular. Since organizational effectiveness is closely linked to the ability of supervisors to direct the activities of employees, these findings are important to executives everywhere.

IS A SUPERVISOR A LEADER?

First-line supervisors are found in all large business and government organizations. They are the men at the base of an organizational hierarchy. Decisions made by the head of the organization reach them through a network of intermediate positions. They are frequently referred to as part of the management team, but their duties seldom seem to support this description.

A supervisor of clerks, tax collectors, meat inspectors, or securities analysts is not charged with budget preparation. He cannot hire or fire the employees in his own unit on his say-so. He does not administer programs which require great planning, coordinating, or decision making.

Then what is he? He is the man who is directly in charge of a group of employees doing productive work for a business or government agency. If the work requires the use of machines, the men he supervises operate them. If the work requires the writing of reports, the men he supervises write them. He is expected to maintain a productive flow of work without creating problems which higher levels of management must solve. But is he a leader?

To carry out a specific part of an agency's mission, management creates a unit, staffs it with a group of employees and designates a supervisor to take charge of them. Management directs what this unit shall do, from time to time changes directions, and often indicates what the group should not do. Management presumably creates status for the supervisor by giving him more pay, a title, and special privileges.

Management asks a supervisor to get his workers to attain organizational goals, including the desired quantity and quality of production. Supposedly, he has authority to enable him to achieve this objective. Management at least assumes that by establishing the status of the supervisor's position, it has created sufficient authority to enable him to achieve these goals—not his goals, nor necessarily the group's, but management's goals.

In addition, supervision includes writing reports, keeping records of membership in a higher-level administrative group, industrial engineering, safety engineering, editorial duties, housekeeping duties, etc. The supervisor as a member of an organizational network, must be responsible to the changing demands of the management above him. At the same time, he must be responsive to the demands of the work group of which he is a member. He is placed in the difficult position of communicating and implementing new decisions, changed programs and revised production quotas for his work group, although he may have had little part in developing them.

It follows, then, that supervision has a special characteristic: achievement of goals, previously set by management, through the efforts of others. It is in this feature of the supervisor's job that we find the role of a leader in the sense of the following definition: *A leader is that person who most effectively influences group activities toward goal setting and goal achievements.*

This definition is broad. It covers both leaders in groups that come together voluntarily and in those brought together through a work assignment in a factory, store, or government agency. In the natural group, the authority necessary to attain goals is determined by the group membership and is granted by them. In the working group, it is apparent that the establishment of a supervisory position creates a predisposition on the part of employees to accept the authority of the occupant of that position. We cannot, however, assume that mere occupation confers authority sufficient to assure the accomplishment of an organization's goals.

Supervision is different, then, from leadership. The supervisor is expected to fulfill the role of leader but without obtaining a grant of authority from the group he supervises. The supervisor is expected to influence the group in the achieving of goals but is often handicapped by having little influence on the organizational process by which goals are set. The supervisor, because he works in an organizational setting, has the burdens of additional organizational duties and restrictions and requirements arising out of the fact that his position is subordinate to a hierarchy of higher-level supervisors. These differences between leadership and supervision are reflected in our definition: *Supervision is basically a leadership role, in a formal organization, which has as its objective the effective influencing of other employees.*

Even though these differences between supervision and leadership exist, a significant finding of experimenters in this field is that supervisors must be leaders to be successful.

The problem is: How can a supervisor exercise leadership in an organizational setting? We might say that the supervisor is expected to be a natural leader in a situation which does not come about naturally. His situation becomes really difficult in an organization which is more eager to make its supervisors into followers rather than leaders.

LEADERSHIP: NATURAL AND ORGANIZATIONAL

Leadership, in its usual sense of *natural* leadership, and supervision are not the same. In some cases, leadership embraces broader powers and functions than supervision; in other cases, supervision embraces more than leadership. This is true both because of the organization and technical aspects of the supervisor's job and because of the relatively freer setting and inherent authority of the natural leader.

The natural leader usually has much more authority and influence than the supervisor. Group members not only follow his command but prefer it that way. The employee, however, can appeal the supervisor's commands to his union or to the supervisor's superior or to the personnel office. These intercessors represent restrictions on the supervisor's power to lead.

The natural leader can gain greater membership involvement in the group's objectives, and he can change the objectives of the group. The supervisor can attempt to gain employee support only for management's objectives; he cannot set other objectives. In these instances leadership is broader than supervision.

The natural leader must depend upon whatever skills are available when seeking to attain objectives. The supervisor is trained in the administrative skills necessary to achieve management's goals. If he does not possess the requisite skills, however, he can call upon management's technicians.

A natural leader can maintain his leadership, in certain groups, merely by satisfying members' need for group affiliation. The supervisor must maintain his leadership by directing and organizing his group to achieve specific organizational goals set for him and his group by management. He must have a technical competence and a kind of coordinating ability which is not needed by many natural leaders.

A natural leader is responsible only to his group which grants him authority. The supervisor is responsible to management, which employs him, and also to the work group of which he is a member. The supervisor has the exceedingly difficult job of reconciling the demands of two groups frequently in conflict. He is often placed in the untenable position of trying to play two antagonistic roles. In the above instance, supervision is broader than leadership.

ORGANIZATIONAL INFLUENCES ON LEADERSHIP

The supervisor is both a product and a prisoner of the organization wherein we find him. The organization which creates the supervisor's position also obstructs, restricts, and channelizes the exercise of his duties. These influences extend beyond prescribed functional relationships to specific supervisory behavior. For example, even in a face-to-face situation involving one of his subordinates, the supervisor's actions are controlled to a great extent by his organization. His behavior must conform to the organization policy on human relations, rules which dictate personnel procedures, specific prohibitions governing conduct, the attitudes of his own superior, etc. He is not a free agent operating within the limits of his work group. His freedom of action is much more circumscribed than is generally admitted. The organizational influences which limit his leadership actions can be classified as structure, prescriptions, and proscriptions.

The organizational structure places each supervisor's position in context with other designated positions. It determines the relationships between his position and specific positions which impinge on his. The structure of the organization designates a certain position to which he looks for orders and information about his work. It gives a particular status to his position within a pattern of statuses from which he perceives that (1) certain positions are on a par, organizationally, with his, (2) other positions are subordinate, and (3) still others are superior.

The organizational structure determines those positions to which he should look for advice and assistance, and those positions to which he should give advice and assistance.

For instance, the organizational structure has predetermined that the supervisor of a clerical processing unit shall report to a supervisory position in a higher echelon. He shall have certain relationships with the supervisors of the work units which transmit work to and receive work from his unit. He shall discuss changes and clarification of procedures with certain staff units, such as organization and methods, cost accounting, and personnel. He shall consult supervisors of units which provide or receive special work assignments.

The organizational structure, however, establishes patterns other than those of the relationships of positions. These are the patterns of responsibility, authority, and expectations.

The supervisor is responsible for certain activities or results; he is presumably invested with the authority to achieve these. His set of authority and responsibility is interwoven with other sets to the end that all goals and functions of the organization are parceled out in small, manageable lots. This, of course, establishes a series of expectations: a single supervisor can perform his particular set of duties only upon the assumption that preceding or contiguous sets of duties have been, or are being carried out. At the same time, he is aware of the expectations of others that he will fulfill his functional role.

The structure of an organization establishes relationships between specified positions and specific expectations for these positions. The fact that these relationships and expectations are established is one thing; whether or not they are met is another.

PRESCRIPTIONS AND PROSCRIPTIONS

But let us return to the organizational influences which act to restrict the supervisor's exercise of leadership. These are the prescriptions and proscriptions generally in effect in all organizations, and those peculiar to a single organization. In brief these are the *thou shalt's* and the *thou shalt not's*.

Organizations not only prescribe certain duties for individual supervisory positions, they also prescribe specific methods and means of carrying out these duties and maintaining management-employee relations. These include rules, regulations, policy, and tradition. It does no good for the supervisor to say, *This seems to be the best way to handle such-and-such,* if the organization has established a routine for dealing with problems. For good or bad, there are rules that state that firings shall be executed in such a manner, accompanied by a certain notification; that training shall be conducted, and in this manner. Proscriptions are merely negative prescriptions; you may not discriminate against any employee because of politics or race; you shall not suspend any employee without following certain procedures and obtaining certain approvals.

Most of these prohibitions and rules apply to the area of interpersonal relations, precisely the area which is now arousing most interest on the part of administrators and managers. We have become concerned about the contrast between formally prescribed relationships and interpersonal relationships, and this brings us to the often discussed informal organization.

FORMAL AND INFORMAL ORGANIZATIONS

As we well know, the functions and activities of any organization are broken down into individual units of work called positions. Administrators must establish a pattern which will link these positions to each other and relate them to a system of authority and responsibility. Man-to-man are spelled out as plainly as possible for all to understand. Managers, then, build an official structure which we call the formal organization.

In these same organizations, employees react individually and in groups to institutionally determined roles. John, a worker, rides in the same carpool as Joe, a foreman. An unplanned communication develops. Harry, a machinist knows more about high-speed machining than his foreman or anyone else in his shop. An unofficial tool boss comes into being. Mary, who fought with Jane, is promoted over her. Jane now gives Mary's directions. A planned relationship fails to develop. The employees have built a structure which we call the informal organization.

> *Formal organization is a system of management-prescribed relations between positions in an organization.*
>
> *Informal organization is a network of unofficial relations between people in an organization.*

These definitions might lead us to the absurd conclusion that positions carry out formal activities and that employe4es spend their time in unofficial activities. We must recognize that organizational activities are in all cases carried out by people. The formal structure provides a needed framework within which interpersonal relations occur. What we call informal organization is the complex of normal, natural relations among employees. These personal relationships may be negative or positive. That is, they may impede or aid the achievement of organizational goals. For example, friendship between two supervisors greatly increases the probability of good cooperation and coordination between their sections. On the other hand, *buck passing* nullifies the formal structure by failure to meet a prescribed and expected responsibility.

It is improbable that an ideal organization exists where all activities are carried out in strict conformity to a formally prescribed pattern of functional roles. Informal organization arises because of the incompleteness and ambiguities in the network of formally prescribed relationships, or in response to the needs or inadequacies of supervisors or managers who hold prescribed functional roles in an organization. Many of these relationships are not prescribed by the organizational pattern; many cannot be prescribed; many should not be prescribed.

Management faces the problem of keeping the informal organization in harmony with the mission of the agency. One way to do this is to make sure that all employees have a clear understanding of and are sympathetic with that mission. The issuance of organizational charts, procedural manuals, and functional descriptions of the work to be done by divisions and sections helps communicate management's plans and goals. Issuances alone, of course, cannot do the whole job. They should be accompanied by oral discussion and explanation. Management must ensure that there is mutual understanding and acceptance of charts and procedures. More important is that management acquaint itself with the attitudes, activities, and peculiar brands of logic which govern the informal organization. Only through this type of knowledge can they and supervisors keep informal goals consistent with the agency mission.

SUPERVISION STATUS AND FUNCTIONAL ROLE

A well-established supervisor is respected by the employees who work with him. They defer to his wishes. It is clear that a superior-subordinate relationship has been established. That is, status of the supervisor has been established in relation to other employees of the same work group. This same supervisor gains the respect of employees when he behaves in as certain manner. He will be expected, generally, to follow the customs of the group in such matters as dress, recreation, and manner of speaking. The group has a set of expectations as to his behavior. His position is a functional role which carries with it a collection of rights and obligations.

The position of supervisor usually has a status distinct from the individual who occupies it: it is much like a position description which exists whether or not there is an incumbent. The status of a supervisory position is valued higher than that of an employee position both because of the functional role of leadership which is assigned to it and because of the status symbols of titles, rights, and privileges which go with it.

Social ranking, or status, is not simple because it involves both the position and the man. An individual may be ranked higher than others because of his education, social background, perceived leadership ability, or conformity to group customs and ideals. If such a man is ranked higher by the members of a work group than their supervisor, the supervisor's effectiveness may be seriously undermined.

If the organization does not build and reinforce a supervisor's status, his position can be undermined in a different way. This will happen when managers go around rather than through the supervisor or designate him as a straw boss, acting boss, or otherwise not a real boss.

Let us clarify this last point. A role, and corresponding status, establishes a set of expectations. Employees expect their supervisor to do certain things and to act in certain ways. They are prepared to respond to that expected behavior. When the supervisor's behavior does not conform to their expectations, they are surprised, confused, and ill-at-ease. It becomes necessary for them to resolve their confusion, if they can. They might do this by turning to one of their own members for leadership. If the confusion continues, or their attempted solutions are not satisfactory, they will probably become a poorly motivated, non-cohesive group which cannot function very well.

COMMUNICATION AND THE SUPERVISOR

In a recent survey, railroad workers reported that they rarely look to their supervisor for information about the company. This is startling, at least to us, because we ordinarily think of the supervisor as the link between management and worker. We expect the supervisor to be the prime source of information about the company. Actually, the railroad workers listed the supervisor next to last in the o5rder of their sources of information. Most surprising of all, the supervisors, themselves, stated that rumor and unofficial contacts were their principal sources of information. Here we see one of the reasons why supervisors may not be as effective as management desires.

The supervisor is not only being bypassed by his work group, he is being ignored, and his position weakened, by the very organization which is holding him responsible for the activities of his workers. If he is management's representative to the employee, then management has an obligation to keep him informed of its activities. This is necessary if he is to carry out his functions efficiently and maintain his leadership in the work group. The supervisor is expected to be a source of information; when he is not, his status is not clear, and employees are dissatisfied because he has not lived up to expectations.

By providing information to the supervisor to pass along to employees, we can strengthen his position as leader of the group, and increase satisfaction and cohesion within the group. Because he has more information than the other members, receives information sooner, and passes it along at the proper times, members turn to him as a source and also provide him with information in the hope of receiving some in return. From this, we can see an increase in group cohesiveness because:

- Employees are bound closer to their supervisor because he is *in the know*.
- There is less need to go outside the group for answers
- Employees will more quickly turn to the supervisor for enlightenment

The fact that he has the answers will also enhance the supervisor's standing in the eyes of his men. This increased status will serve to bolster his authority and control of the group and will probably result in improved morale and productivity.

The foregoing, of course, does not mean that all management information should be given out. There are obviously certain policy determinations and discussions which need not or cannot be transmitted to all supervisors. However, the supervisor must be kept as fully informed as possible so that he can answer questions when asked and can allay needless fears and anxieties. Further, the supervisor has the responsibility of encouraging employee questions and submissions of information. He must be able to present information to employees so that it is clearly understood and accepted. His attitude and manner should make it clear that he believes in what he is saying, that the information is necessary or desirable to the group, and that he is prepared to act on the basis of the information.

SUPERVISION AND JOB PERFORMANCE

The productivity of work groups is a product; employees' efforts are multiplied by the supervision they receive. Many investigators have analyzed this relationship and have discovered elements of supervision which differentiate high and low production groups. These researchers have identified certain types of supervisory practices which they classify as *employee-centered* and other types which they classify as *production centered*.

The difference between these two kinds of supervision lies not in specific practices but in the approach or orientation to supervision. The employee-centered supervisor directs most of his efforts toward increasing employee motivation. He is concerned more with realizing the potential energy of persons than with administrative and technological methods of increasing efficiency and productivity. He is the man who finds ways of causing employees to want to work harder with the same tools. These supervisors emphasize the personal relations between their employees and themselves.

Now, obviously, these pictures are overdrawn. No one supervisor has all the virtues of the ideal type of employee-centered supervisor. And, fortunately, no one supervisor has all the bad traits found in many production-centered supervisors. We should remember that the various practices that researchers have fond which distinguish these two kinds of supervision represent the many practices and methods of supervisors of all gradations between these extremes. We should be careful, too, of the implications of the labels attached to the two types. For instance, being production-centered is not necessarily bad, since the principal responsibility of any supervisor is maintaining the production level that is expected of his work group. Being employee-centered may not necessarily be good, if the only result is a happy, chuckling crew of loafers. To return to the researchers' findings, employee-centered supervisors:

- Recommend promotions, transfers, pay increases
- Inform men about what is happening in the company
- Keep men posted on how well they are doing
- Hear complaints and grievances sympathetically
- Speak up for subordinates

Production-centered supervisors, on the other hand, don't do those things. They check on employees more frequently, give more detailed and frequent instructions, don't give reasons for changes, and are more punitive when mistakes are made. Employee-centered supervisors were reported to contribute to high morale and high production, whereas production-centered supervision was associated with lower morale and less production.

More recent findings, however, show that the relationship between supervision and productivity is not this simple. Investigators now report that high production is more frequently associated with supervisory practices which combine employee-centered behavior with concern for production. (This concern is not the same, however, as anxiety about production, which is the hallmark of our production-centered supervisor.) Let us examine these apparently contradictory findings and the premises from which they are derived.

SUPERVISION AND MORALE

Why do supervisory activities cause high or low production? As the name implies, the activities of the employee-centered supervisor tend to relate him more closely and satisfactorily to his workers. The production-centered supervisor's practices tend to separate him from his group and to foster antagonism. An analysis of this difference may answer our question.

Earlier, we pointed out that the supervisor is a type of leader and that leadership is intimately related to the group in which it occurs We discover, now, that an employee-centered supervisor's primary activities are concerned with both his leadership and his group membership. Such a supervisor is a member of a group and occupies a leadership role in that group.

These facts are sometimes obscured when we speak of the supervisor as management's representative, or as the organizational link between management and the employee, or as the end of the chain of command. If we really want to understand what it is we expect of the supervisor, we must remember that he is the designated leader of a group of employees to whom he is bound by interaction and interdependence.

Most of his actions are aimed, consciously or unconsciously, at strengthening membership ties in the group. This includes both making members more conscious that he is a member of their group) and causing members to identify themselves more closely with the group. These ends are accomplished by:

- making the group more attractive to the worker: they find satisfaction of their needs for recognition, friendship, enjoyable work, etc.;
- maintaining open communication: employees can express their views and obtain information about the organization
- giving assistance: members can seek advice on personal problems as well as their work; and
- acting as a buffer between the group and management: he speaks up for his men and explains the reasons for management's decisions.

Such actions both strengthen group cohesiveness and solidarity and affirm the supervisor's leadership position in the group.

DEFINING MORALE

This brings us back to a point mentioned earlier. We had said that employee-centered supervisors contribute to high morale as well as to high production. But how can we explain units which have low morale and high productivity, or vice versa? Usually production and morale are considered separately, partly because they are measured against different criteria and partly because, in some instances, they seem to be independent of each other.

Some of this difficulty may stem from confusion over definitions of morale. Morale has been defined as, or measured by, absences from work, satisfaction with job or company, dissension among members of work groups, productivity, apathy or lack of interest, readiness to help others, and a general aura of happiness as rated by observers. Some of these criteria of morale are not subject to the influence of the supervisor, and some of them are not clearly related to productivity. Definitions like these invite findings of low morale coupled with high production.

Both productivity and morale can be influenced by environmental factors not under the control of group members or supervisors. Such things as plant layout, organizational structure and goals, lighting, ventilation, communications, and management planning may have an adverse or desirable effect.

We might resolve the dilemma by defining morale on the basis of our understanding of the supervisor as leader of a group; morale is the degree of satisfaction of group members with their leadership. In this light, the supervisor's employee-centered activities bear a clear relation to morale. His efforts to increase employee identification with the group and to strengthen his leadership lead to greater satisfaction with that leadership. By increasing group cohesiveness and by demonstrating that his influence and power can aid the group, he is able to enhance his leadership status and afford satisfaction to the group.

SUPERVISION, PRODUCTION, AND MORALE

There are factors within the organization itself which determine whether increased production is possible:

- Are production goals expressed in terms understandable to employees and are they realistic?
- Do supervisors responsible for production respect the agency mission and production goals?
- If employees do not know how to do the job well, does management provide a trainer—often the supervisor—who can teach efficient work methods?

There are other factors within the work group which determine whether increased production will be attained:

- Is leadership present which can bring about the desired level of production?
- Are production goals accepted by employees as reasonable and attainable?
- If group effort is involved, are members able to coordinate their efforts?

Research findings confirm the view that an employee-centered supervisor can achieve higher morale than a production-centered supervisor. Managers may well ask what is the relationship between this and production.

Supervision is production-oriented to the extent that it focuses attention on achieving organizational goals, and plans and devises methods for attaining them; it is employee-centered to the extent that it focuses attention on employee attitudes toward those goals, and plans and works toward maintenance of employee satisfaction.

High productivity and low morale result when a supervisor plans and organizes work efficiently but cannot achieve high membership satisfaction. Low production and high morale result when a supervisor, though keeping members satisfied with his leadership, either has not gained acceptance of organizational goals or does not have the technical competence to achieve them.

The relationship between supervision, morale, and productivity is an interdependent one, with the supervisor playing an integral role due to his ability to influence productivity and morale independently of each other.

A supervisor who can plan his work well has good technical knowledge, and who can install better production methods can raise production without necessarily increasing group satisfaction. On the other hand, a supervisor who can motivate his employees and keep them satisfied with his leadership can gain high production in spite of technical difficulties and environmental obstacles.

CLIMATE AND SUPERVISION

Climate, the intangible environment of an organization made up of attitudes, beliefs, and traditions, plays a large part in morale, productivity, and supervision. Usually when we speak of climate and its relationship to morale and productivity, we talk about the merits of *democratic* versus *authoritarian* climate. Employees seem to produce more and have higher morale in a democratic climate, whereas in an authoritarian climate, the reverse seems to be true or so the researchers tell us. We would do well to determine what these terms mean to supervision.

Perhaps most of our difficulty in understanding and applying these concepts comes from our emotional reactions to the words themselves. For example, authoritarian climate is usually painted as the very blackest kind of dictatorship. This is not surprising, because we are usually expected to believe that it is invariably bad. Conversely, democratic climate is drawn to make the driven snow look impure by comparison.

Now these descriptions are most probably true when we talk about our political processes, or town meetings, or freedom of speech. However, the same labels have been used by social scientists in other contexts and have also been applied to government and business organizations, without it, it seems, any recognition that the meanings and their social values may have changed somewhat

For example, these labels were used in experiments conducted in an informal classroom setting using 11-year-old boys as subjects. The descriptive labels applied to the climate of the setting as well as the type of leadership practiced. When these labels were transferred to a management setting, it seems that many presumed that they principally meant the king of leadership rather than climate. We can see that there is a great difference between the experimental and management settings and that leadership practices for one might be inappropriate for the other.

It is doubtful that formal work organizations can be anything but authoritarian, in that goals are set by management and a hierarchy exists through which decisions and orders from the top are transmitted downward. Organizations are authoritarian by structure and need; direction and control are placed in the hands of a few in order to gain fast and efficient decision making. Now this does not mean to describe a dictatorship. It is merely the recognition of the fact that direction of organizational affairs comes from above. It should be noted that leadership in some natural groups is, in this sense, authoritarian.

Granting that formal organizations have this kind of authoritarian leadership, can there be a democratic climate? Certainly there can be, but we would want to define and delimit this term. A more realistic meaning of democratic climate in organizations is the use of permissive and participatory methods in management-employee relations. That is, a mutual exchange of information and explanation with the granting of individual freedom within certain restricted and defined limits. However, it is not our purpose to debate the merits of authoritarianism versus democracy. We recognize that within the small work group there is a need for freedom from constraint and an increase in participation in order to achieve organizational goals within the framework of the organizational movement.

Another aspect of climate is best expressed by this familiar, and true, saying: actions speak louder than words. Of particular concern to us is this effect of management climate on the behavior of supervisors, particularly in employee-centered activities.

There have been reports of disappointment with efforts to make supervisors ore employee-centered. Managers state that, since research has shown ways of improving human relations, supervisors should begin to practice these methods. Usually a training course in human relations is established; and supervisors are given this training. Managers then sit back and wait for the expected improvements, only to find that there are none.

If we wish to produce changes in the supervisor's behavior, the climate must be made appropriate and rewarding to the changed behavior. This means that top-level attitudes and behavior cannot deny or contradict the change we are attempting to effect. Basic changes in organizational behavior cannot be made with any permanence, unless we provide an environment that is receptive to the changes and rewards those persons who do change.

IMPROVING SUPERVISION

Anyone who has read this far might expect to find *A Dozen Rules for Dealing With Employees* or *29 Steps to Supervisory Success*. We will not provide such a list.

Simple rules suffer from their simplicity. They ignore the complexities of human behavior. Reliance upon rules may cause supervisors to concentrate on superficial aspects of their relations with employees. It may preclude genuine understanding.

The supervisor who relies on a list of rules tends to think of people in mechanistic terms. In a certain situation, he uses *Rule No. 3*. Employees are not treated as thinking and feeling persons, but rather as figures in a formula: Rule 3 applied to employee X = Production.

Employees usually recognize mechanical manipulation and become dissatisfied and resentful. They lose faith in, and respect for, their supervisor, and this may be reflected in lower morale and productivity.

We do not mean that supervisors must become social science experts if they wish to improve. Reports of current research indicate that there are two major parts of their job which can be strengthened through self-improvement: (1) Work planning, including technical skills, and (2) motivation of employees.

The most effective supervisors combine excellence in the administrative and technical aspects of their work with friendly and considerate personal relations with their employees.

CRITICAL PERSONAL RELATIONS

Later in this chapter we shall talk about administrative aspects of supervision, but first let us comment on *friendly and considerate personal relations*. We have discussed this subject throughout the preceding chapters, but we want to review some of the critical supervisory influences on personal relations.

Closeness of Supervision: The closeness of supervision has an important effect on productivity and morale. Mann and Dent found that supervisors of low-producing units supervise very closely, while high-producing supervisors exercise only general supervision. It was found that the low-producing supervisors:

- check on employees more frequently
- give more detailed and frequent instructions
- limit employee's freedom to do job in own way

Workers who felt less closely supervised reported that they were better satisfied with their jobs and the company. We should note that the manner or attitude of the supervisor has an important bearing on whether employees perceive supervision as being close or general.

These findings are another way of saying that supervision does not mean standing over the employee and telling him what to do and when and how to do it. The more effective supervisor tells his employees what is required, giving general instructions.

COMMUNICATION

Supervisors of high-production units consider communication as one of the most important aspects of their job. Effective communication is used by these supervisors to achieve better interpersonal relations and improved employee motivation. Low-production supervisors do not rate communications as highly important.

High-producing supervisors find that an important aid to more effective communication is listening. They are ready to listen to both personal problems or interests and questions about the work. This does not mean that they are *nosey* or meddle in their employees' personal lives, but rather that they show a willingness to listen, and do listen, if their employees wish to discuss problems.

These supervisors inform employees about forthcoming changes in work; they discuss agency policy with employees; and they make sure that each employee knows how well he is doing. What these supervisors do is use two-way communication effectively. Unless the supervisor freely imparts information, he will not receive information in return.

Attitudes and perception are frequently affected by communication or the lack of it. Research surveys reveal that many supervisors are not aware of their employees' attitudes, nor do they know what personal reactions their supervision arouses. Through frank discussion with employees, they have been surprised to discover employee beliefs about which they were ignorant. Discussion sometimes reveals that the supervisor and his employees have totally different impressions about the same event. The supervisor should be constantly on the alert for misconceptions about his words and deeds. He must remember that, although his actions are perfectly clear to himself, they may be, and frequently are, viewed differently by employees.

Failure to communicate information results in misconceptions and false assumptions. What you say and how you say it will strongly affect your employees' attitudes and perceptions. By giving them available information, you can prevent misconceptions; by discussion, you may be able to change attitudes; by questioning, you can discover what the perceptions and assumptions really are. And it need hardly be added that actions should conform very closely to words.

If we were to attempt to reduce the above discussion on communication to rules, we would have a long list which would be based on one cardinal principle: Don't make assumptions!

- Don't assume that your employees know; tell them.
- Don't assume that you know how they feel; find out.
- Don't assume that they understand; clarify.

20 SUPERVISORY HINTS

1. Avoid inconsistency.
2. Always give employees a chance to explain their action before taking disciplinary action. Don't allow too much time for a "cooling off" period before disciplining an employee.
3. Be specific in your criticisms.
4. Delegate responsibility wisely.
5. Do not argue or lose your temper, and avoid being impatient.
6. Promote mutual respect and be fair, impartial, and open-minded.
7. Keep in mind that asking for employees' advice and input can be helpful in decision making.
8. If you make promises, keep them.
9. Always keep the feelings, abilities, dignity and motives of your staff in mind.
10. Remain loyal to your employees' interests.
11. Never criticize employees in front of others, or treat employees like children.
12. Admit mistakes. Don't place blame on your employees, or make excuses.
13. Be reasonable in your expectations, give complete instructions, and establish well-planned goals.
14. Be knowledgeable about office details and procedures, but avoid becoming bogged down in details.
15. Avoid supervising too closely or too loosely. Employees should also view you as an approachable supervisor.
16. Remember that employees' personal problems may affect job performance, but become involved only when appropriate.
17. Work to develop workers, and to instill a feeling of cooperation while working toward mutual goals.
18. Do not overpraise or underpraise, be properly appreciative.
19. Never ask an employee to discipline someone for you.
20. A complaint, even if unjustified, should be taken seriously.

NOTES

www.ingramcontent.com/pod-product-compliance
Lightning Source LLC
Chambersburg PA
CBHW082210300426
44117CB00016B/2752